CLACKAMAS LITERARY REVIEW

2016
Volume XX

Clackamas Community College
Oregon City, Oregon

CLR
CLACKAMAS LITERARY REVIEW

Managing Editor
Matthew Warren

Associate Editors
Marlene Broemer   Trista Cornelius   Sean Davis

Trevor Dodge   Jeff McAlpine   Nicole Rosevear

Amy Warren

Assistant Editors & Designers
Becca Aguilar   Joe Ballard   Julia Berezhnoy

Tom Boggess   Eric Bronson   Janel Brubaker

Jack Eikrem   Ashley Goolsby   Rebekah Lee

Delilah Martinez   Victoria Marinelli   Colton Merris

Shilo Niziolek   Alexa Short   Natalie Spitzer

Chelsea Thiel

Cover Art
Where Buffalo and Unicorn Once Roamed by Katie Todd

The Clackamas Literary Review is published annually at Clackamas Community College. Manuscripts are read from September 1st to December 31st and will not be returned. By submitting your work to *CLR*, you indicate your consent for us to publish that work in print and online. This issue is $10; issues I–XI are $6 if ordered through *CLR*; issues XII–XIX are available through your favorite online bookseller.

Clackamas Literary Review
19600 Molalla Avenue, Oregon City, Oregon 97045
ISBN: 978-0-9796882-8-7
Printed by Lightning Source
www.clackamasliteraryreview.org

CONTENTS

PROSE

POSSIBILITY

Thanks to
Ryan Davis, for his tireless work,
and to
Trevor Dodge, for his unwavering vision

Editors' Note

*P*ublishing. It is how ideas are shared—writer with reader, editors with audience. It's the process for creating, from story, artifact. Books allow us to explore. We read to listen. To learn. To react. To connect. And that's intimate. This artifact is our connection to the past, alive always in the present.

Writers spark this connection by capturing ideas with a key stroke, or a sliding pen. They make black ink waltz across white dancefloors, curving, crossing, dotting, slashing—until letters become words and words become voice. And that is the *CLR*. Voices from around the world have danced their way into this book—some floating across the page to an orchestra, others gyrating to the bass of hip-hop. Nothing is out of place.

And that's the beauty of the *CLR*—unity. Caffeinated students drag themselves out of bed twice a week with one thing on their minds: *publishing*. It's uncommon to publish a book in ten weeks the way we have. We are college students. We are friends. And we are editors: arguing over word count, font, slush-piles, styles, back matter, word choice, order, art. Our contrast is how we collaborate. Our collaboration *is* publishing.

Now it's your turn to participate. Listen to these writers. Read. Learn. *React.*

How to End an Affair

Cindy King

As soon as you catch his eye, let it go,
and when he has your ear, quit listening.
If that doesn't work, fall back into your body
whenever gravity returns. If nothing beats
the bars of his ribs, your pulse will no longer sing blue.
The air will cool, and make room for you, resume
its routine in your lungs. Permit cigarettes to burn
into ash, and there will be no words for *smoldering.*
Ice will let down the empty wine bottles; they'll sink to new lows
in the tub. And when sweat forgives your forehead,
your conscience will harden like wax over honey. Only then
will it finally be morning, the sun giving up the horizon,
searching windows in succession as it rises. Expect your
faces to gray in its searchlight. Stars will stagger
up to night's penthouse and the moon will unzip
the sky's blue. Once the freight of your talk is unloaded,
switch rails, whistle with the empty boxcar of your mouth.
You can be sure that the washcloth will forget your face,
the bath towel will free his waist, and your shapes will be shaken
from pillows. Once you latch the door behind him,
watch the TV drama shrink to a single point of light.

secrets / lies

Toni Hanner

he shines / & black & / wriggles electrified / fish a snake he / thrashes
inside my lost body / i tell her / yes / when she asks i / tell her / yes she
kindness / hair a dark river / empty of children

the lie / slithers / i write my history in numbers / & languages / iron /
copper / a field freshly harrowed he was / my heart

secrets abide
i am afraid of compassion

Spring Fever

Frank Rossini

in this month of the green
apostle
before beebuzz and pollen
when horny toms
fan tails & gobble
gobble after flirty hens
when the day's promise
is the promise of work the need
to hold the wild
in hand to prune
mow dig haul lift push
pull   on this morning
my boots
& gloves gather
the last
heat from night's
dying
fire
a flicker half-
heartedly chases
towhees from the suet   squirrels chatter
through down-

pours
the dog groans
as she dreams
by the door
& like Jesus the morning after
a good Friday I lie
quietly
waiting
for the stone to roll
from my eyes
& I plan
how I'll move
a rose   maybe plant
an oak in the north field
a maple
in the east   how I might
dig a small pond   stack
a stone wall build
a rain house where
my wife & I sip
tea around a tight fire & watch
in winter
storms gather
then flow from the hills shaking
the bamboo sometimes
bowing
them to the ground   I plan
how I will
keep up with this land as it stirs

sprouts erupts
into an unruly throng
their song setting trees
to blossom their dance luring
even a bloodied
Jesus to rise
from death & walk
one last time
this earth in glorious riot

hand me my gloves
my fiery boots
I
am ready

Foreclosure

Maya Hickman

Empty the contents of your hands,
let the ceramic have its firework moment with the ground.
Back away from the broken fragments.

Unpack it.
Hand it over.
Flip the cushions off the couch,
turn the trash bin over outside
Then clear the kitchen drawers right into it.

Take the clothing down from careful hangers, into a box
walk through the open field to the river
behind the house.

Dump them where the river curves,
waves on its way by.
They will swell and flow.

Empty the fridge.
Don't worry about the nice glass Tupperware.

Throw it all in a black bag for the
trash pick up,
turn off the humming machine,

Rip the knobs from the cabinets.

Turn off the upstairs lights.
Take the narrow staircase a last time.
Off with the kitchen light.

Leave the front door open
jump the short front steps
Walk away from it.

Child Care

Margaret Malone

When Maxine left she took the station wagon, some clothes, and her curling iron. Everything else I got. That first night, I smoked half a pack of stale Pall Malls that I found in her bedside table, and I hadn't smoked since the Navy. I threw up right after. So now I'm smoking again. Not so smart at my age, but who's left to care? Hal said that I had to keep moving, that was the trick. Forward motion, he said. That's when he had the idea about me watching those kids.

Hal's a security guard at the community center, and the two of us were sitting on a green bench at the park there, watching all these dogs running around while their owners stood on the grass holding leashes. Hal was in his uniform. It was the first time I'd left the house for something other than orange juice or a TV dinner in a month. The world felt like sandpaper against my skin.

Hal said the deal was for Friday nights. "Fridays, it's AA in the gymnasium," he said, "and some of the drinkers, you know, they need to bring their kids to those meetings. But, they're not allowed in."

"Yeah, that'd be disruptive," I said.

"No, not that," he said. "Because of confidentiality."

Then I said, "What happened to the guy who did it before?"

"Jimmy. He got a gig working the door at a bar on Olympic."

I told Hal I don't know. I mean, it didn't sound all that great.

"What am I supposed to do with the kids?" I said. "I don't know kids."

Hal said, "Just keep them busy at the playground here. Keep them safe until the meeting's over."

I didn't say anything. I watched a big black dog pee onto the trunk of a tree.

Hal said, "It pays about forty bucks depending on donations and the meetings are about an hour or two, depending on if they're talking after." He was slow getting up from the bench.

"You're old," I told him.

Hal said, "Let me talk to someone. If it's not you, it's gonna be some other guy so you might as well say yes."

That first Friday night I showered and put on fresh slacks. Don't ask me why I wanted to look good for those damn kids. I parked the truck in the lot and I didn't see Hal anywhere. The community center was all lit up from the inside and the main double doors were propped open, a few folks starting to head in.

I walked through the open doors, my shoes squeaking on the gym floor. A bald guy wearing a nametag that said Stu sat behind a table. I told him I was Frank and I was here to watch the kids, and he said, you're Hal's buddy, and I said, yup, Frank, that's me. He said that it's usually only three or four kids, and thanks for helping out, and I better go wait outside on the grass to round them up before heading off to the playground.

It was pretty dark out by then and sure enough there were a couple of kids hanging out on the front lawn, a bigger one, a boy with a lot of ears, and a littler one, a girl with messy pigtails. I asked if they had parents in the meeting.

The bigger one said, "Our mom." He pointed to a white lady wearing a too-big sweatshirt smoking a cigarette in front of the open doors.

I said, "So Jimmy normally watches you right?"

The littler one, the girl, said, "Where's Jimmy?"

I said, "I guess I'm Jimmy now. My name's Frank."

The boy with big ears said he was Andre and his sister was Amanda and *frank* is what his grandpa calls a hot dog.

Amanda said, "How old are you?"

"Old," I said. "Very old."

She said she was eight and Andre was nine and what did I like better cats or dogs.

"I don't know. They're both okay," I said. "You think anyone else is coming?"

Andre said, "We have to wait for Rudy. He always comes with his mom and sometimes his mom's boyfriend too."

"I like Rudy," Amanda said.

After a couple weeks, I settled into the routine pretty quick. When everyone's arrived we walk around back to the park where there's a playground. It's dark as hell by the time we're out there and as soon as we get to the play area they take off their little shoes and socks so they don't get sandy. I stand by the oak tree under one of the park's streetlamps and smoke cigarettes and make sure the kids don't fall or hurt one another too much until the meeting is over, and then I bring them back to the grass in front of the gym's double doors where I hand the kids back to their parents and collect my forty bucks. Sometimes I think about taking my shoes off too, the sand between my toes might feel good, but Maxine always said I had ugly old man feet and I don't want to scare the kids. Sometimes I push them on the swings, or wait at the bottom of the slide. Tag. Hide-and-Seek. Red-Light, Green-Light. One time Amanda didn't want to play anything at all, so we stood under the streetlamp, her small hand in mine, and we watched the boys rough-housing in the sand.

Problem was, I got to thinking about the parents in the meetings, their kids out here killing time in a dark playground, all of us waiting around for those folks to get their shit together. There's no way a kid could understand.

So tonight I bring something easy. I think maybe it could help. I don't worry about them telling. Nobody lies like the children of drunks.

We hide in the caterpillar tunnel over the sand, the one that connects the red plastic slide with the wobbly bridge. I have to duck my head to get inside and my bones creak when I bend my body to fit. The four of us sit in a row, squashed together.

Something easy, no bourbon, or schnapps.

I pull the two cans from the inside pocket of my jacket. I pop a can open, take a sip, and pass it down the line.

"I don't think we're supposed to have that," Rudy says.

"It's okay. I'm going to show you something," I say. "Take a sip, if you want."

Rudy nods his small head and smiles. Amanda doesn't say anything. She gets real quiet. Rudy is just holding the can; he hasn't sipped it yet. I pop the other can open for me.

"Andre," I say. "You started drinking yet with your friends?" I ask. "It's okay. You can tell me." He shakes his head and gives me a look like, don't be ridiculous. Rudy hands the can off to Andre and he puts his little mouth up to the can and drinks. His face scrunches up. "This is nasty," he says. He takes another little sip.

"Not too fast," I say. "Not too much."

I love these damn kids. It's easy to misunderstand. "Everyone warm enough?" I ask. Sure, I give them a cigarette. I light it, just one; we share. The smoke wafts around in the tunnel.

Amanda starts coughing. "I have asthma," she says.

"Sorry," I say. I put it out. "Okay, that was a bad idea. Sorry."

They take nibble-y sips from their beer. Andre and Rudy passing the can back and forth.

Andre says, "Isn't beer supposed to be cold?"

Rudy says, "It kind of tastes gross."

"I brought pretzels," I say. To coat their stomachs, but also to help set the scene. Rudy rips the bag open, loud. He shoves a handful in his mouth and passes it down the line. I want them to understand. I try to explain what it is—how people talk in bars; the way, when you're drinking, it's like the people you're drinking with are your real friends; and how sometimes it feels like you are safer with them than you are your own family.

What it really is I guess is people just listen different in bars, they hear things better, and pretty soon things that are true you didn't even know were true just pop right out of your mouth.

In the best times, I tell them, it's like a magic bubble happens, like you're deep in space, and there's no sound but whatever true thing you're saying, and the person you're talking to is really hearing you. They're listening to your stories like they are important, like they are their stories too.

The three of them, their little faces are looking up at me. Footsteps and a jangly dog collar on the nearby path, closer and then farther away.

They say they want to hear one of my stories. My neck starts to cramp. I don't know what to say. I take a sip of warm beer.

I tell them about fishing in the little creek behind my uncle's place when I was their age and how I would stand on the muddy bank in my bare feet just hoping I wouldn't catch anything because nothing was better than the feeling of sun on my arms and the cold creek on my feet and not needing to do anything at all but wait for nothing to happen. I keep talking and eventually I get around to Maxine and how I can't say what really happened there but that, even with everything that seemed to go wrong, there was one time when we were camping in our trailer in Yosemite and the sun wasn't all the way up yet and I could just make out the tops of the campground trees against all that granite and in that moment the smell of pine and dust was just about the best thing ever of all time.

I stop talking and take a drink again. The side of the can says the beer is straight from the Rockies. That makes me melancholy. "Maxine and I camped in the Rockies once," I say.

I start to recall things that I don't want to get into. I'm just beginning to learn to forget and I don't want to undo all that hard work. These damn kids, the three of them staring at me. It's too much.

"Pass the pretzels," I say.

"You're holding the pretzels," Andre says.

"Someone else go," I say.

"I don't want to go," Amanda says. "Can I have a pretzel?"

I clear my throat and pass the bag down to her. "It's about knowing things, friendship, like that," I say. "Andre?"

He takes a quick sip of beer from the can he's sharing with Rudy. He says one time just after Halloween but before Thanksgiving he was stuck late after school because his mom forgot to pick him up.

He bummed around the playground for a bit, he tells us, but he didn't know what to do. So he started walking to the grocery store.

"I know the lady who works with the fruit and vegetables. She's my neighbor. She's let me use the phone before, the one in the back by the big walk-inside refrigerator." But once he got to the store, he says, he didn't feel like going inside. It was getting cold out, he says, "But I didn't want to go home."

Instead he sat outside on the automated mini carousel and wished he had a quarter to make it go. Then a kid came along.

"He had food stuck on his face, like dried peanut butter or something, but he had a quarter," Andre says.

The messy kid sunk his twenty-five cents in the slot and smiled at Andre. "Then he said to me, 'You wanna be friends?' and I said no. It sounds mean but, I don't know, I *didn't* want to be his friend. He seemed weird." They rode around in quiet circles for a minute until their time ran out.

"Like that?" he asks me.

I tell him, good job. Great job, kid. I try to shift position so I'm not so scrunched up in the tunnel. My cramped neck is really killing me now and my feet are starting to get cold. "Who's next?" I say.

Amanda says, "I don't want to go." Her voice sounds tired.

"You don't have to, honey," I say. "Rudy? It's getting late. You want a turn?"

Rudy says he doesn't want any more beer but can he tell a story and I say, sure thing. He tells us about a time when he burnt his hand on the stove while making hot chocolate.

His mom's boyfriend didn't think Rudy's accident required much attention so the boyfriend continued to finish his crossword puzzle at the kitchen table and Rudy says that's when he decided to hate him forever. Is that good, he says?

I don't like that story.

I think how one of the best things about camping with Maxine was the part about being somewhere that wasn't home. I ask the kids if they would rather be somewhere else.

"I know I would," I say.

Amanda says yes, she's getting cold.

So we pile into my truck, the old Chevy pick-up that Maxine and I used to haul the trailer from park to park. The engine turns over and that truck growls and rumbles underneath us. I crank the heater up and Amanda says that's better.

When they ask in a minute where we're going I will tell them the truth, that I don't know. The picture develops: we're all driving up the coast, stopping to eat burgers and soft-serve at a roadside stand, days at the beaches, nights around a campfire. North through California, Oregon, through Washington, even farther, whatever it takes, into Canada, Alaska, until they see. I'll show them how quiet it can be, how much space there is. For the first time in a long time a spark lights up inside me. This is just what I need, a chance to finally get back on the road.

Those damn kids, their three faces looking up at me.

If they want to go back, they can just say the word. It's up to them.

The truck grumbling underneath us.

Home or away, I'll say. It's your call.

The cake's no longer a cake,

Jonathan Greenhause

Occupied by air where there was
      a paper box
where the cake was, & the people
      who ate the cake
are no longer people, are
      occupied by air
inside a wooden box where people
      used to be.

Things lose their characteristics
      so easily, with
such inevitability in the face
      of the seconds
accumulating with such ferocity,
      devouring
the hallowed space where they
      used to be.

So what was cake is now air,
      & what was us
is also air, & what the nation was
      is what our dreams

were & what our concept of
      eternity is,
all these things occupied by air
      occupying

a universe, where if we look
      far enough
we'll see how these things lose
      their specific
characteristics, becoming part
      of everything,
a place where we end up going
      & being

regardless of whether we admit it.

Bullet Fish

Ruth Foley

That year, I began sleeping like a shark
finned. I sank, discarded, into something
far away from morning. My trail shimmered
behind me as I torpedoed down—I didn't
know what it beckoned or who would
follow it. I was a submarine gone inert,
its crew unbreathing, their faces porcelain
as if they waited for the pin to drop. I was
the pin. I was an airplane cabin plummeting
wingless to the seabed. Plumes of silt would
luff when I landed, and I would welcome
their gust and bluster. I was ready to be centered
in a sand fountain, ready for someone to
make a wish. Shorn, I might have been
a bullet fish moving forward, only forward,
water freshening across my gills as I
came alive again, restored in the sluice of this
false current, waking to brandish
what was missing. I thrashed the places
where my muscle used to be. Each exhaled
stream was my last before I found
the ocean floor, the silica settling around me

like winter's dust beaten out of a carpet,
unglimmered and wretched, and acknowledged
I was as useless as I would have been in air.

What to Do When You Don't Know What to Do

Todd McKie

He's a red-haired man who's stopped looking in mirrors. Not shaving hasn't helped, of course, but there's something screwed up about his eyes, too.

The man sits at a kitchen table, sliding a cigarette in and out of his mouth with his left hand. His right hand rearranges the objects on the table: coffee cup, ashtray, paper napkin, checkbook. He knows he's smoking, but he may not be aware of how he's moving things around, changing their relationship to one another.

The man crushes out his cigarette, picks up the checkbook. He flips through it, sighs, puts it down. He slides the ashtray closer to the napkin and looks out the window, fixing his eyes on the house next door until its shingles blur. He hears a bus, a radio, birds chirping. Nearby a phone rings and rings. *Why the hell doesn't somebody answer that?* thinks the man. He blinks and turns from the window when he realizes it's his phone.

"Hello?"

"Philip, it's you!" says his friend Isabel.

"Who were you expecting?"

"The phone kept ringing, so I…"

Philip closes his eyes, holds the phone at arm's length and sticks out his tongue.

"Philip? Are you there?"

"I thought that had been established."

"So, you're alone?"

"No, Isabel, there's a big party going on over here, the place is packed."

"Can I come over right now?"

"I'll slip into something pretty."

Isabel, wearing a pink tee shirt and green shorts, kisses Philip's cheek. She carries a small white box. "Can I come in?"

"Oh, yeah, sorry."

"Stop with the 'sorry,' already."

"Sorry."

They both laugh. He steps aside and Isabel walks past him and down the hall. Philip follows, wondering if Isabel read somewhere that baggy shorts give the illusion of shapely legs. When they get to the kitchen she puts the white box on the table.

"Philip, I saw the newspaper. Are you okay?"

"Tip-top. Never been better. What's in the box?"

"I stopped at Barsamian's. I was afraid you weren't eating."

"I'm eating."

"You're smoking!" says Isabel, looking at the ashtray.

"It's the same as eating, cigarettes are very nutritious."

Isabel opens the box. Two slices of coffee cake. "These are really good," she says. "Bobby loves these things."

"Bobby *looks* like he loves them."

"And you look like you're not eating at all."

"Isabel, c'mon, I'll eat, I'll stuff myself, they'll have to take me out of here with a crane, for Christ's sake."

They sit and drink coffee and eat cake from pale yellow plates. They talk about the weather, how hot it is for early April.

"Philip, I'm sorry I couldn't be there. Rachel's in a play at school and I'm helping with the costumes. Yesterday was the dress rehearsal."

"Isabel, you don't have to apologize. What's the play?"

"Rumpelstiltskin."

"Is it good?"

"It's a class play, it's just kids."

"How's Rachel?"

"It's just a tiny part. She's got a rubber chicken and when the King passes by she curtsies and hands him the chicken. The King thanks her and she says, 'You're welcome, Sire.'"

"A star is born! Jill loves the theater, she's always complaining we never go. How much are the tickets?"

"Philip, there aren't any tickets—it's at ten o'clock in the morning!"

"That's pretty early, maybe we'll skip it." He lights another cigarette and looks out the window.

"Earth to Philip."

"When he was little I used to sit right here and watch him playing outside. I could see the top of his head if he was digging in the dirt or whatever. One time he and his friend Matt built a fort out of plywood and some old boards. It had rusty nails sticking out all over the place and a concrete block balanced on top. I made them pull it apart. I should have let him have his fort."

"Philip, I'm so sorry."

"We're all sorry. That's what we are—a sorry lot."

Philip looks out the window again, but this time he looks up, up above the house next door. He watches a cloud drift across the sky. When it disappears, he turns toward Isabel. He contorts his face into an exaggerated smile and cocks his head.

"Philip, that's really grotesque. Stop, that's so creepy!"

He pokes his nose twice, each time making a honking noise.

"What are you doing? If you could see yourself you wouldn't think it was so funny."

"It's not funny, Isabel, it's sad. I'm a sad clown, laughing on the outside, but…"

"Stop it!"

He relaxes his face. The smile is gone.

"How about going to the studio? Bobby's picking up Rachel, so I've got the whole day."

"Isabel, I don't remember how to make stuff. I don't even have clay."

"Okay, we'll get some. Where do you buy your clay?"

"In Waltham. But you don't want to drive all the way out there, do you? Just to get clay?"

"Sure I do! We can have lunch at one of those little restaurants on Moody Street. Bobby and I went to a really good Thai place out there. C'mon, my treat. We're going to fatten you up. You can't just sit here all day."

"The thing is, I *can* just sit here. I'll read the goddamn paper."

"Bobby went crazy when he saw the Globe this morning."

"You should have seen Jill at the hearing. She stood up and yelled at one of the lawyers. She called him a 'sleazy bastard.'"

"Bobby said he was going to call you. This was at six o'clock in the morning. I said, 'Don't you dare call Jill and Philip.'"

"He could have called. Jill was still asleep, but I was up."

"Did you try those pills?"

"Isabel, I can't. I don't want to get fucked up. I know, I'm totally fucked up already, but I don't want to get more fucked up."

"You've got to sleep. You're fucked up because you can't sleep. Bobby takes them and he's like you—he won't take an aspirin. They have absolutely no side effects."

"Okay, if I can't sleep tonight I'll try one."

"Promise?"

"Scout's honor."

Philip gathers up the cups and the plates smudged with cake and takes them to the sink. He picks up the ashtray and dumps the butts into a waste basket in the corner. *I'll do this*, he thinks, *and then I'll do something else, and if I do enough of these things, this day will end.*

Philip buys three hundred pounds of red clay and lifts the fifty-pound boxes into the back seat of Isabel's Toyota. They drive along Route 16 until it crosses the river, turn onto Moody Street and park. Philip jumps out and lights a cigarette; Isabel won't let him smoke in her car. He looks up and down the street while Isabel puts quarters in the meter.

"Are you hungry?" she asks. "I'm starved."

"Watching me buy that clay must have been pretty exhausting. Then you had to watch me carry it out to the car—no wonder you're hungry."

"I offered to help."

"Isabel, it's a manly thing. Men have to do these things. And women have to watch. Then the women drive the men to the chiropractor. It's nature's way."

They sit at a red table by the front window of the Thai Palace. "What are you going to have?" asks Isabel, scanning the menu. "Bobby and I had some duck thing. Do you like duck?"

"Too greasy. Quack, quack."

"You know what sounds yummy? Shrimp with Basil and Garlic."

"Let's get that. And Pad Thai," says Philip.

"Perfect. The shrimp thing has three stars. Is that too hot?"

"Isabel, I can't eat it unless it *is* hot."

"I forgot, you're Mister Spicy, aren't you? Bobby is such a wimp. He thinks Italian food is too hot."

The waitress, in a white blouse and blue skirt, comes to the table. She's a pretty Thai girl with short black hair. She smiles while she takes their order. Philip watches her walk to the kitchen.

"Isn't she adorable?" says Isabel.

"Her shirt is the cleanest, saddest piece of clothing I've ever seen," says Philip.

"You notice the weirdest things."

"You didn't notice her shirt?" asks Philip.

"I only saw a white blouse, but you're the artist—you get paid to notice those things."

The girl brings their lunch and a Diet Coke for Isabel, a Singha beer for Philip. Isabel digs right in. Philip eats a couple of forkfuls then just moves the noodles and the shrimp and the peppers around on his plate. He drinks his beer from the bottle.

"Philip, you're driving me nuts pushing that food all over the place. Put some in your mouth."

"I ate some, I ate a lot, really."

"Right. Rachel's a bigger eater than you are, and we think she might have an eating disorder."

"How can Rachel have an eating disorder? She's seven years old, for Christ's sake."

"Eight."

Philip waves to the waitress and holds up his empty bottle. He knows Isabel is giving him a dirty look and for a second or two the thought gives him great pleasure.

"What's so darn funny?" asks Isabel.

Philip shakes his head. He turns to watch the girl bring his beer. The way she's holding the little tray with the bottle on it, her smile, her hair, that white shirt, every piece of the picture is breaking Philip's heart. He's trying so hard not to cry that when she sets the beer in front of him he cannot speak. His lips shape the words "Thank you." The water that fills his eyes has blurred his vision, so when the waitress leaves the table Philip sees only a white shape bobbing away from them.

"I wish there was something I could do," says Isabel. "That sounds pathetic, doesn't it? But, really, what can I do?"

"You're buying me lunch. That's something." Philip puts the bottle to his mouth and takes a long cold swallow. "That's something right there."

"When's the next court thing? Bobby and I are definitely coming."

"There's another hearing in two weeks. It's strange, though, to sit right behind them. I wanted to jump over the railing and hit them with a chair. But then, it turned out that Jill was the one who lost control."

"It's hard to picture Jill losing control," says Isabel.

"It's hard to picture *any* of it. After Jill yelled at the lawyer, the judge called a recess and told the District Attorney to make Jill shut up. The DA told Jill he understood her anger but, please, be quiet. Even after that, out in the hallway, she said something to another lawyer."

"What did she say?"

"She said, 'How do you sleep at night, you lying son of a bitch?'"

Philip finishes his beer and Isabel pays for lunch. The waitress brings the change and sets it on the table in a little dish. She says, "Thank you. I hope you will come again."

"It was delicious, everything was so good," says Isabel to the girl.

"My favorite thing was your blouse," says Philip.

The girl looks confused. Her eyes narrow for a second and then, still bewildered, she smiles.

Isabel takes the turnpike into Boston. She's a fast driver. Philip rolls down his window and closes his eyes. The wind whistles and pushes against his face. On this warm day Philip thinks of snow, wet mittens, hot chocolate. He sees a boy making angels in the snow. "I'm flying in the snow," says the boy. "Look at me, I'm flying away in the snow."

When the first spatters of blood hit the snow, Philip opens his eyes. He rolls up the window. He makes a fist and presses it into the middle of his chest. He says, "Are we there yet?"

"I thought you were asleep. Were you asleep?"

"No such luck."

When they reach his studio building in the South End, Philip piles the clay onto the loading dock, walks up to the second floor. He rings for the freight elevator and brings it down to the street. He heaves the boxes into the elevator. Isabel hops in, and they ride in the dusty cage up to Philip's fifth-floor studio.

"I'll make some coffee," says Philip.

Philip busies himself in the little kitchen in a corner of the studio. Isabel stands at the far end of the room, looking at the platters, bowls, and vases that are lined up on wooden shelves. Some are plain, but others are decorated, and a few have been glazed. There are vases with primitive faces drawn on them, crude black strokes marking eyes, noses, mouths. There are bowls decorated with colorful fruits and vegetables.

"Philip, these are beautiful. You've got a lot of new things."

"They're from before. I had to pack some things for a show in Chicago, but since then I haven't been in here at all."

"You have the world's neatest studio. I never saw so many shelves in my whole life."

"Willy helped me build those shelves," says Philip. "He painted the ceiling and the floor. He worked down here for a couple of weekends. I paid him a hundred and fifty bucks."

"Oh, Philip, what's happening in this world?"

"He thought he was rich. I remember one day, when he was helping me, we went over to the fish place for lunch. He bought me lunch. He said, 'Dad, I'm buying.'"

Isabel digs in her pocketbook for a Kleenex. She wipes it across her eyes and blows her nose. Philip pours the coffee into two cups and opens the door of the miniature refrigerator.

"I've got some milk, but I think its been in here for a while." He lifts the carton and sniffs it. "Whew! That's ripe. Here, smell this." He holds the milk out toward Isabel.

"Why do people always do that?" says Isabel, backing away.

"Do *what*?"

"When people smell something really bad, really nauseating, why do they always want you to smell it too?"

"Suit yourself," says Philip. He pours the milk into the sink.

Philip spreads a sheet of newspaper on his dusty work table, sets their coffee cups down next to a headline that says *Bruins Batter Toronto.*

"Thanks for today," says Philip.

"What did *I* do? You don't need to thank me."

"Hey, you bought me lunch. You tricked me into coming down here."

"I didn't trick you. You wanted to come."

"Isabel, you tricked me, but thanks anyway."

"Okay, you're welcome. Now, how about tomorrow?"

"What do you mean, 'how about tomorrow?' Who says I want to do this every day?"

"I'm not talking about every day, just until you…you know."

"Get back on my feet? Jesus, am I that bad?"

"Philip, you can't just sit around your apartment smoking all day."

Philip looks up at the ceiling, at the complicated pattern of beams and pipes and corrugated tin. He sees a boy on a ladder. A boy with a paintbrush in his hand, white paint in his hair.

"I do more than smoke, Isabel, I do lots of different things. I stop doing them when you come over, but I do plenty of things."

"Like?" says Isabel. "Name something else you do."

"Well…I pay bills, we get lots of bills. And we're still getting cards. I have to read those."

They sit in silence, sipping their coffee. Philip smokes one cigarette after another. The sun slides down and the studio takes on an amber glow. Their shadows stretch and blur in the fading light. Philip looks at his watch. "I guess we better go," he says.

"It's getting dark already," says Isabel.

"It's a dark day in April," says Philip. He makes his hands into claws and circles them around in front of Isabel's face. He makes his voice sound like Peter Lorre: "It's a dark and dangerous day."

"Philip, please don't do that. Be normal."

"Okay. I wouldn't do it for anyone else, but for you, Isabel, I'll be normal. Just this once."

Philip gets up and moves around the table to Isabel. He takes her hand and leads her out of the studio. They walk down five flights of stairs. There is no sound but the tap of their shoes on the concrete steps and the muffled hum of traffic on the turnpike.

Philip lets himself into the apartment. There's a light in the kitchen and he moves toward it. He calls out softly, "Jill? Are you home?" There's no answer, but Jill's keys are on the table next to a pile of mail and her green sweater is lying over the back of a chair.

Philip leaves the kitchen, goes through the living room into the back hall. The first door on the left is open. Philip touches the door frame gently, like touching someone's face. A streetlight shines some light into the room and Philip sees Willy's bed, his desk and, glinting silver and gold, Willy's baseball trophies.

Philip walks to the bedroom he shares with Jill. The door is shut, but there's a strip of yellow light beneath it. He opens the door slowly. Jill is lying on her back with her mouth open, breathing softly. The blanket is pulled up to her chin. Jill's reading lamp is on, but beyond the ragged circle of light, everything is dark. A book, half in light and half in shadow, lies open on the blanket. Philip picks up the book, a book that Betty, who works in Jill's office, gave them. The book is called *What to Do When You Don't Know What to Do.* Oh, brother, thinks Philip. He lays the book on Jill's bedside table and switches off the light. He leaves the room and—carefully, quietly—closes the door.

In the kitchen Philip pours himself a glass of water and chugs it down in one long gulp. He wipes the water from his chin and picks up the pile of mail. There are a couple of bills, a catalog of occult books and CD's, and something from Long's Funeral Home. There are also three fancy envelopes, the ones that bring cards and notes. One of these envelopes has been opened and from it Philip pulls a card with a drawing of geese, or maybe ducks, flying up from a pond. Around the pond are pine trees and the sun is setting. Or rising. Inside, in loopy handwriting, is a note from Jill's aunt Eleanor, who lives in Wisconsin.

Eleanor writes some of the usual things, but she has an odd way of using words and capital letters. She uses phrases like *In His Infinite Wisdom* and *God's Blue Print* and *Eternal Rest,* the kinds of phrases that Philip, although he knows they are meant to comfort, is tired of reading. But then Eleanor goes on to write about a long-ago Fourth of July picnic. She mentions something Willy, who was four years old that summer, said, and how it still makes her chuckle *to This Very Day.* Willy and his cousins were kicking a soccer ball around and Willy fell and got a big grass stain on his white shorts. *Do you Remember what he said?* writes Eleanor. *Mom, I wrecked my Short Sleeve Pants!* She says she can see that picnic, and hear Willy's voice, as if it were *Yesterday.* Eleanor ends the note by saying that Jill and Philip are in her *Thoughts And Prayers.*

Philip slides the card back into the envelope. He can barely breathe and he can't swallow. When he turns out the overhead light the apartment is completely dark. He stumbles to the bedroom and, sitting on the edge of the bed, takes off his shoes. Then Philip, fully dressed, climbs under the covers. He lies on his back and listens to the sound of Jill's breathing. He tries to match the rhythm of his breath, in and out, to hers.

Philip imagines himself an Indian Yogi, wearing just a loincloth, in a frigid limestone cave. The Yogi hears a loud siren and suddenly he's a regular man again, a man who is breathing too quickly, a man with a hole in his heart.

Philip reaches over to the bedside table. His fingers close around a small bottle of pills. He shakes it. The siren fades. He shakes the bottle again and the siren disappears. And then, because this device seems to work, seems to be useful to a man in a tight spot, Philip shakes the bottle once more. This last time just for the pure sad hell of it.

Bucket of Water Wife

James Valvis

A mistake to make her my bride.
She was too malleable, too willing
to change to any shape to please me.
If we touched, she engulfed my hands,
spilled down my arms.
Mornings I'd wake up drenched,
as if I suffered night sweats or enuresis.
Once I left her unattended
and the maid stuck a mop in her.
Bugs landed on her arms and drowned.
What kind of children would she raise?
Little puddles for people to step in?
We finally took the honeymoon.
On the pier, I told her my plans.
She cried, but there was never a time
she wasn't crying, never once
her life wasn't tears, and she agreed
it was best she return to her kind.
I felt awful dumping her into the sea,
yet she dispersed immediately.
I shook my head, blinked at the sun,
and having survived that disaster

I started for land thinking
love would be easier from now on.
But then on the way home
I filled the bucket with rocks.

See Saw

Mary Miller

My cookies were lumpy and craggy. He pointed at one and said, that looks like a mountain, and then he pointed at another and said, that looks like something else. I forget. I was high. He fixed them, molded them into perfect little cookie-like forms while I watched.

It'll be like they came from the grocery store, he said.

I don't like grocery store cookies, I said.

Then he said something about how they would taste homemade but look like grocery store cookies, which was the best of both worlds. After that he got out his see saw and polished his new bowling ball. He had debated between gold and black but had gone with black.

I don't know why the guy said this thing was a gimmick, he said, it's awesome.

Probably cause it was on *The Big Lebowski*. They have to separate themselves from it.

He licked his finger and rubbed a spot.

Is it shiny enough? I asked.

Not quite, he said, looking at me.

I had spent most of the day doing things for him while he was at work but he didn't mention them or they hadn't been done to his liking. I'd left the gym early to start dinner even though I would have been perfectly happy eating crackers and cheese on the counter. I could have gone to my house but I didn't want to say *fuck you I hate you I never want to talk to you again* because then I would want to talk to him again, probably the next day, or the day after that, and guys tended to take breakups seriously. They had also maintained their friendships and had people to hang out with, people who would drag them out of their houses and take them dancing.

He checked Instagram to see how many people had liked his bowling ball. He posted things and felt validated or invalidated. I looked at it with him sometimes and observed the things he liked. He didn't like people unless they were babies. That was the only thing I could say for sure. But otherwise all of the other hearts he doled out seemed random, arbitrary.

He went to the bathroom so I invited the dog onto the couch with me. She was uncomfortable cuddling so I had to make her: the way to do this was to pretend to pick her up—she didn't like to be picked up—and then she'd jump onto the couch herself. She put her paws on my chest, one folded under. I straightened it. She was like fine. We looked into each other's eyes for a long time while I petted her. It was so easy to look into her eyes. There was no judgment, no bigotry or carelessness or meanness or worry that her love wouldn't be returned or that she was unlovable. I could hardly look into my boyfriend's eyes. In them was every fight we'd ever had and every time he wanted me to be a girl who made homemade cookies like grocery store cookies and I looked at him with eyes that remembered every time I'd had sex with him when I hadn't wanted to and all the rest of it.

Then he was next to me, pushing the dog off and taking another bong hit. I had only seen the bong last week. Months and months with no bong and then bong. Streaked dirty at the bowl. I hadn't seen one since college. I really liked the bong. I liked the efficiency of it, and how I didn't need more and more.

I fixed myself a plate of cookies and a cup of cow milk. He only drank almond milk. I liked almond milk fine but it wasn't cow milk. I imagined thousands of almonds being squeezed and wondered how almond milk—if thousands of almonds had been involved—only cost three dollars. He wasn't ready to eat cookies. They were perfectly baked and I appreciated that he had bothered to shape them. They really were quite nice. This was how things went. He would show me how to do something "the right way," and I would be irritated and angry and then I would realize that his way was better.

Why Poets Are Hated After Dark

Alex Andrew Hughes

She tells him to knock it off. She wants
to go to sleep but she can't when he flicks
on the lamp to scribble some thought,
to scratch some note, to begin a poem
he wants to finish tomorrow. She hates
the nightly on-off, on-off, and hates the
waiting, wondering if there is another clever
thought out there, falling from the stratosphere.

She tells him to knock it off, and he does,
sort of, but she can't bear to see him
walk across the house to write nothing
but a line or two. She buys him a
flashlight to use because she thinks it will help,
to let her sleep while he worries about being
less creative in the morning, but soon she hates
the way the flashlight clicks and comes alive
on quiet summer evenings. She grumbles
and turns over, trying to block the glow
and written tone of the massive firefly,
as the animal beats its wings and takes flight
against the breeze of mediocrity—

She tells him to knock it off and go to bed.
It will all be there tomorrow, and if some of it
vanishes, she will not love him the less.

She tells him to knock it off, not by saying
anything, but by the sounds of her turning over
and staring toward the morning, where she will
read of what beauty she missed yesterday.
A part of her hates being married to a poet who
cannot stop chasing fireflies, but
over time, though she would never say so,
she learns to love hating it.

Why I Refused to Swim with the Manatees

Ruth Foley

My first mistake was of separation.
It was easier to call them sacred
than me unworthy—even straining,
head to hip over starboard, one hand
to the water, I knew that much.
What was lost: not my palm across
a sunken flank, not the fresh water
clearing the cove to brackishness.
A boy stood on the dock, hosing
a pod of three, each shifting between
itch and thirst. Me half in the boat.
Easy to claim we belonged apart.
My second mistake was believing
I had nothing to pour into them.

If I had slipped the Zodiac side,
what would have become of me?
Sunken mammal heart, flippering
as I traced the propeller scars,
whipshot across all three backs—
I, who had spent my life upside-down,
a *Cassiopea* unstinging, carried from

crab to crab. Once truly submerged,
I knew, I would not be able to raise
myself back over the rubber shell
of the boat with my shrunken arms.
Who could serve such a head in her
hands and then return? How could I
have helped but raise my head to drink?

Before We Forget Ourselves

Dov Weinman

let us caress the clouds
and hold the moon in our hands,
howl curses into sideways rain,
place faith in mountain passes.
let wet hair paint cold floorboards,
shed our clothes
like extra skin we've outgrown
and crouch, animal-like
in front of the wood stove.
warm more than our skin
in front of flame,
and then it is you and me,
the storm,
the fire,
and then finally darkness.
we'll run along nurse logs,
naked as the riverbed,
and offer ourselves
to whatever might take us.

Love, from J & S

Jamie Iredell

Dear Tom,

We're here! It's late summer, the days hot and sunny, the nights so warm we sleep with the windows open and the zephyrs rush down off the mountainsides and through the valley, rustling the aspens so they whisper to us, and the pine trunks and branches bend and moan like old men. It's beautiful! We're excited about the move and this lovely location high in the mountains.

Love, from J & S

Dear Tom,

We took jobs at the ski resort in the heart of the valley, but training doesn't begin for another month, so this gives us plenty of time to get settled. Didn't bring much—we own so very little. This is good as the cabin is rather small. It must be the oldest building on the street, most the other cabins having only recently been built. They're not really "cabins," but these behemoths of stone and glass, with antlered chandeliers suspended from vaulted foyers, which we can see through the all-glass facades. No wonder our rent is so cheap! The cabin is quaint and cozy, all knotted pine walls, an old buck trophy hammered into the living room wall. The landlord's this little old man who drove up from the lowlands to show us the place. He seemed eager for renters, and was enthusiastic about our degrees and our plans to ski through the winter. He had these funny bushy eyebrows and a shifty, twitching smile. Anyway, I'm rambling. We're doing great!

Love, from J & S.

Dear Tom,

The aspens have shifted from green to a vibrant yellow and the scrub willow stems burned red, the mule ears shriveled up, and the warm mountain breezes have cooled. The clouds that gather and hover over the snowpacked peaks march across and dump inches of rain, swelling the creek that runs past the front of our cabin. Soon, we'll be starting our new jobs so we're trying to take advantage of what little free time we have left. Still beautiful here. We're trying to take advantage of any good remaining weather!

Love, from J & S

Dear Tom,

We explored the woods behind the cabin and discovered an old dirt logging road. It had been some time since anyone drove the road and shoots of grass and weeds had grown into the eroded ruts. We followed the road a short distance up the mountain and when the road summited, it opened on a beautiful view of the valley, with the lone road wandering past the meadow and the golf course up to the empty ski resort parking lot. We looked at this and the surrounding mountains—all tinged gold in autumn—for a minute before we continued on the road, where it turned deeper into the woods.

The road came to an old shuttered cabin. The windows had been hastily boarded, the boards themselves weathered, the nails rusty. The stained and tattered remains of an easy chair and a couch (the springs showing in places) had been abandoned outside the building. Let me tell you, the feeling we got once we'd discovered this place was a cold and barren one, despite the hike up the mountain that sweated us out. We marched around the old place, keeping our distance, but it wasn't long that the feeling got the better of us and we hurried out of there, back down the road and through the woods to our cabin where we built a fire in the fireplace. And though it did take some time, we eventually again got warmed through. Very weird. Ever had that feeling about a place?

Love, from J & S

Tom,

We started work and met our coworkers who were all very nice, all locals, or seasonals like us, but the other seasonals have worked at the resort for a number of winters. Everyone wanted to know how we were liking life in the mountains so far. It's a different world, they say, a different pace to life, a whole new attitude. We agree. It's nothing like life back in the city! They wanted to know all about that, so of course we told them about you—all those parties we always had! Missing you! We told them about our cabin and they said that our landlord had been offered tons of money many times to sell the place to a developer, but the old guy wouldn't cave. It was weird, they said, because renters never stayed for more than a month. We were the first in years who planned to stay at least a half year. It is weird, since the place is perfectly pleasant. His loss! We get the cabin and the valley for ourselves—and we're loving it!

Love, from J & S

Dear Tom,

The other night we got ready to meet up with friends at a bar in the valley. We'd been unusually testy with one another, batting hasty responses to questions. After we showered and dressed and left off our slights, we headed out of the bedroom. We walked down the hallway, barely noticing the fact that the sliding door to the hallway closet was wide open, though we hadn't opened it. It was only after we'd passed and hurried out of the cabin, gotten into the car, and driven away that we both said we felt the same thing: that as we passed the closet there had loomed the shape of a man standing in the gloom, all of it made darker by the dark of the hallway in the early evening. Our descriptions of the man—despite each of us seeing him only on the periphery of our vision—matched. He was tall and thin and prominent of the cheekbones, with thick and high-arched black eyebrows. WTF, right? We had only wanted to hurry out of the house at the feeling when we passed the closet, and we had not wanted to return to see if it was but an illusion. When we retreated home later that evening we found the closet door closed as it ought to have been, and upon opening it we discovered nothing out of the ordinary. Just the vacuum and broom, the hot water heater and the washer and dryer, just as always. But the feeling was the same one from when we found the cabin on top of the mountain, and all that night, though we piled the blankets on our bed and built a fire and turned up the heater, we could not seem to get warm.

Weird, I know.

With love,

J&S

Dear Tom,

The first snow fell Halloween night. It had been a clear but windy and chilly day. The few locals with children walked about the neighborhood streets, and the little princesses and witches and ghosts held out their bags and pillowcases and hollow plastic pumpkins for the candy that we and others handed out. Just before dark the clouds engulfed the valley and fat flakes sifted down from the white sky. Some of the children and their parents scurried home while others remained in the street, where we joined them, packing the sticking snow into meager balls that we hurled at one another. It was all good fun till one of us took a snowball to the face. We've been fighting. Stupid things, like about doing the dishes, or picking up dirty clothes tossed by the bedside. We don't have anything better to do? By dark a few inches of snow coated the trees, the road, and the ground, and, spent from fighting and shivering, we hustled inside and got a fire going. After dinner, when we needed more wood from the pile outside, we stepped beyond the covered hall that protects the path to the front door from snow, and all of the footprints that we'd made earlier had been filled. Except that they weren't, or at least ours were, and there were fresh prints. The footprints weren't in the street, but circled our cabin and stopped in front of the windows where the toes faced the window glass, as if whoever had made the prints was trying to look inside. With a flashlight, we followed the prints all around the cabin, but the prints didn't come from anywhere, nor did they leave across the back or front yard. It was like the footprints just appeared at our cabin and whoever made them walked around and peered in at us, then vanished. Weird, I know. We're doing okay.

 With love from J & S

Dear Tom,

 Merry Christmas! We hope you and yours are all well and that you're snuggled up safe and warm and that you're enjoying your holiday. We've decided to ask around, to find out what we can about our little cabin here in the mountains. This was after repeated calls to our landlord met no response, and he never returned our calls after the messages we left. He still cashes our rent checks though, albeit late in the month, though we're always on time with the payment. More strange things have been happening. We've awakened in the night, paralyzed with fear, the chill running up our spines though we lay unable to move while visions of eyes through the windows watch us. We read up about sleep paralysis. We found dead animals all about the outside of the cabin. Sometimes it was just a dead bird, a scrub jay that snapped its neck somehow, flown into the side of the house. Then one morning we found a fawn, completely unharmed, but stiff and dead, inexplicitly lying in the snow in front of the cabin when we left for work, as if a cat had hunted it down and left it there for us to find, but there were no puncture marks—or any other discernible harm—on the body. One morning we found quite a few animals: birds, a beaver, squirrels, and moles, and all of the animals externally appeared to be unharmed: but all deceased. When we told our coworkers about this they nodded at us gravely. Such things were common during the winter when many animals ran out of food. They panicked, attracted by the smell of the garbage humans produced. When we tell people about the man we thought we saw in the closet, or about the footprints around the cabin, everyone thinks we're just imagining it. They must think we're totally losing it. Seriously, WTF?

Anyway, with love, J & S

Dear Tom,

Our problems keep getting worse. We've needled each other over stupid shit, like who took the trash out and left the bear guards down so that as we picked up emptied cans of tuna and submarine sandwich wrappers and coffee filters from the snowed-in driveway we sounded like the gears of a whining small car straining its way up a steep hill. We fought like this till the aforementioned cans of tuna went flying, tossed at one another. Our fights have gotten worse: a lamp tossed against one of the living room's knotted pine walls where it shattered. A fist went through a front window, required four stitches. We spent almost thirty bucks at the hardware store getting new glass cut to replace what we' broke. It seems like this move was a bad idea. I don't know if we'll make it through.

Love, S

Tom,

The snow's piled high on the valley floor and the ski season's in full swing, and each weekend brings hordes from the lowlands, masses that fill the lifts and the bars and restaurants and the little road in the valley. The traffic suffocates us. But in the late afternoons we have the mountains to ourselves and the snow's perfect, even ungroomed, and we traverse the trails in swift swinging motions and the chill air burns our cheeks red. We've been doing better and the skiing no doubt has helped. The evenings we fill with hot baths and glasses of red wine. The fire crackles in the fireplace while the television drones till we fall asleep.

Wish you could be here with us! Maybe visit?

Love, from J & S

Oh Tom,

It was one of those nights when everything seemed perfect then again we started fighting, about what neither of us remembers. All that matters is that we ended up in the bedroom, each of us packing bags to leave, both of us threatening suicide—yes, suicide, it got that bad, I know—should one of us leave. There were knives involved. No one got cut, but our poor, poor clothing. Much of it met its demise, shredded in our anger and tossed out the front door and out an open window. How that window had been opened on such a wintry night we'll never know. But eventually we calmed and talked and we picked up the pieces and closed the window and tried to find a way to sleep. We were nearly asleep when a tapping sounded on the front window. It came so soft that we weren't sure that we heard what we heard. But there it was: tap, tap, tap tap tap. Outside we found a young woman, inappropriately dressed for the season. She was very thin, and she wore only a thin white cotton dress—more like a nightgown—that fell to her ankles. She quietly pleaded for us to help her. How could we not? We implored her to come inside, to sit by the fire and get warm. Her breath spewed clouds, but she would not come inside and she would not let us touch her, even when we offered our jackets and a blanket. She insisted that she needed a ride into the heart of the valley. She said she couldn't stay, that we needed to get going. It was only a mile into the valley center from the cabin, and the resort was equipped with emergency medical supplies for the skiers who might potentially harm themselves on the slopes. Rather than fight with her we got the car started and she climbed into the front seat. It was then we noticed that she was barefoot and that her feet had whitened from the cold, her toes swollen and red, in some places patched with black—sure signs of frostbite. On the short ride into the valley the woman informed us that she lived in a cabin not far from ours, on the top of the mountain. She told us that she and her husband had had an argument, for he had been drinking. He'd been drinking all winter. They were running out of food, but her husband refused to work or to hunt (yes, we thought that was weird, too). Of course, we thought of the cabin we'd found up there last fall, but it looked as though no one had lived there for many years. The woman told us how, in a drunken rage her husband had begun destroying their home, tossing their furniture into the snow. He threatened to kill the woman, so she had run. She ran through the woods losing her boots—which she'd not had time to lace up and tie before she left—when a snowdrift wrenched them from her feet. Ours was the first cabin she found. She said it was the winter that drove her husband to act so. It always did. The winter closed in, and it made everyone up here crazy, the woman said. There was little we could offer in response. We felt what that woman felt. It was in us, whatever it was that she and her husband lived. It had filtered into our bones, some ooze we soaked in. This, the mountains. What had become of her had become of us. We parked in front of the resort's first aid station, which runs twenty-four/seven, as it's the only emergency medical aid in this part of the mountains for miles around. While the woman let herself out of the car on her own, she insisted that now she would be fine, that we not accompany her inside. So that was that. We returned to our cabin. It was only then that we thought about the potentially murderous husband, wherever he was, somewhere out there on the mountain, drunk and reeling after the wife that fled him. She'd said that their cabin sat directly behind our own, and what if, we said. We checked to make sure that the windows and doors were bolted and locked and though we stayed up late, spooked, nothing ever happened, and eventually we fell asleep. The next day at work we asked the EMT's if the night shift had any info about the woman, but they looked at us blankly and said that the night had been uneventful. There was no woman. No one had been treated for frostbite and had not for many years. WTF do you do with all of that? Goddamn. Otherwise, we're hanging in here, trying to keep it together.

Love, J&S

Dear Tom,

Things are bad. I'd like to say nothing happened for the rest of the winter. But I'd be lying. For so long we harbored ill will towards one another. Whatever brought it about—the move from the city to this valley in the mountains, our seclusion, our combatting personalities, whatever—it consumed us. We kept on, alternately fighting, often violently, swallowing whole bottles of pills and puking most of them up. I'm so sorry to tell you all this. We smashed and replaced more windows, we tossed whole pieces of furniture into the snow, trying hard, so hard, to keep our actual hands off of one another. At one point an axe and couch met one another. Another time fire somehow found it's way into an argument. We've always come down from our fights, the love of asking, begging for forgiveness, granting of said forgiveness, making up, then basking in each other's love. It was never like this before we moved here. Wish you were here to distract me, or maybe just to give us some reprieve, but we know it's far, far away.

Love,

S & (I suppose) J

Dear Tom,

It's been awhile since I wrote, but we made it through the winter and we're still okay. Sorry for the long absence. In spring, after the snowmelt, we were rearranging the woodpile outside the cabin when we noticed the face marks on the windows. We made out the oils that skin from the face and hands had left on the cold glass: the hard line of a brow, a nose pressed, the mouth, the hands cupped around so that whoever it was might see inside. Someone tall and with high cheekbones had stood at the windows at the rear of the cabin, looking in at us. Each of us accused the other of spying but we pretty much left it at that. An old fight, for sure. We let it go. Got over it. Now that things are better, what do you think about a visit? It's beautiful here in the spring. The meadow wildflowers are blooming. There's still snow. The creeks are high with water and fat with trout. You'd love it!

Love from J & S

Dear Tom,

We explored behind our cabin, trying to cross country. You won't believe what we found: there is a copse of trees, some snow still left from what must've been a thick bank: a pair of women's boots. But they were old old. Like, they looked like they'd been made a hundred years ago but had been left out there just this winter. You can imagine what we were thinking. We kept on and again found the the old logging road that we discovered last fall and it led us just like before up the mountain. Our crunching boots made the only prints in what was left of the snow. Again we encountered a majestic view before the road turned deep into the woods where it should have terminated at the dilapidated cabin, but now there was no cabin. We found a clearing where some structure must have once stood, but it had long since vanished. Some of the trunks of the older pines that bordered the clearing bore scorch marks. We crunched around in the melting snow and spied new sprigs of spring grass shot up through the shallow cover, and after digging a little we found beneath the snow the blackened coals of a wood structure that had once stood in the spot. Whatever had burned here had burned long ago. And again that cold and empty feeling reeled into us and pervaded our insides. But this time we felt no urgency to get out of there. The sun scoured what remained of the snow and it was chilly but pleasant and soon we caught sight of sand lilies peeking out, their petals as white as the landscape. And the bright red of the flowering snow plant erupted from the shaded depths of pine groves. It was cold here, full of death, but there was life too. And it is like that for us here in the mountains. The others call us locals. We hiked back down the mountain, returned to our cabin where we didn't bother to try to get warm. We have fought and made up and fought and have done so ever since. We're doing just great.

Love, from J & S

Dear Tom,

Summer and fall came and went so quickly! We've missed you. We linger about our mountain retreat, haunting up what we can, haha. We're occasionally bothered by the presence of some others—a high cheekboned man with ill temper, a child and her barefoot mother, a family of four, wide eyed and spooked at night, pulling their bed covers to their chins and sometimes over their heads. Silly people. But they left and others replace them, and then those too make their departure. The cycle continues. But we're good. We're here and it doesn't look like we're leaving any time soon. We just wish you'd find some time to visit.

With love, from J & S

Still Life with Weekend, Ulysses, Laundry, Second Thoughts

Ed Taylor

Saturday, at last; may be harbor
but ringed by hounds, who sound
off with extreme prejudice—so

cut this world loose, just do
your house work, dude;
do not take that call;
          after all, *machine wash
cold*: an odd imperative for care
of delicates, the small clothes
now in a row, those flags
on a line—the wife shapes,
sinuous in seawind,
teasing Ithaca's itches,

while you, old dog, watch,
dream a way to the dark sedan
bowmen cannot fathom,
          and a clean getaway

Dropping In

Asha Dore

The first time I dropped in on a half pipe, I started off strong and ready, balancing the wheels of my skateboard on the metal lip of the ramp. I leaned in, but my legs stiffened, sent the skateboard flying sideways. The concrete curled up and smacked me in the shoulder. I slid down. Stared up at the sky, throbbing. Bright. I sat up in the belly of the pipe. The belly, the cave. I was so hungry. My arms shook. My hands found each other, my fingers pulsing over the veins of my wrists, blood-drum, sharp sprout from the skin of my shoulder. Someone squirted water over my shoulder to wash out the blood, the pinkish water sliding down my arm, the water and blood and my thirst. I drank from the bottle. Let the liquid lean into the rough dark of my slope, the bowl of me, the decline.

In a dream, I follow Dad to Antarctica where he lives underground. A group of baby boomers tunneled a city under the ice. In the dream, I climb a snow dune to find a secret doorway, a lever pulled by lifting a dirty tennis shoe. A chute opens. I slide down a dark tunnel and land in a cafeteria. Everyone eats sushi. Everyone wears ball caps. Everyone wears eyeliner. Everyone smiles. Across the room, a guy takes off his ball cap and turns away, but I see his hair, dark, dark dirt with those weird lilts of light, sun pulled threads, the youngest strands. It's Dad. I follow him. I can hear him breathing. I can hear the back of his

Birkenstocks sliding against the cement. I can't catch up with him. His face is blurry.

Dad had been dead 887 days when I bought my first skateboard. I could barely ride down the sidewalk. I popped my board into my hand and walked over every curb, every crack.

Afterward, the A/C was broken in my apartment, so a group of us went on a search through the neighboring apartment buildings. When we found a pool, I lost my shoe climbing over the gate and swam in my underwear while my friends folded themselves into cannon balls or crossed their arms, arched their backs and fell backward into the pool like corpses. We left our skateboards in a pile on the other side of the fence. Clothes sticking to wet summer bodies, we left, found another pool, this one empty except for the spray paint on the sides. Words like Fuck! Fuck! Fuck! and Live Young Die Free and a scribbled drawing of a duck, a cow, an anarchy symbol, an egg.

I found a boy there, his body a fracture like mine. Our bodies dipping in and out of concrete waves. I set my board up at the bottom of that empty pool. I skated in wide circles, working my way up. The boy dropped in.

Dad's a missing person, not dead. In the beginning of the dreams, I find a clue. A voicemail full of breathing. A motorcycle idling. A sock. I set off on a bus or on the back of a giant bird or a dragon. I find him sleeping under an overpass, covered with flattened cardboard boxes. Or, driving a flat boat, fishing the Florida swamp.

Usually, I don't find him at all. I find his houses, his dwellings: A wide, southern kitchen, Jimmy Buffett's voice wheeling out from a cassette player on the counter. Or a dented trailer in Alabama filled with the mechanical innards of the fire alarms Dad used to sell, their plastic shells broken and scattered like he tore them in half, pulled their guts out, and left again. Or a sleeping bag. A tent. A hotel room. An empty suitcase.

950 days. I let go of my apartment. I moved from house to house, sleeping on porches or couches or floors. Some nights, I filled my backpack with paint, skated to a row of darkened office buildings, hinged the wheels of my board between my backpack and my shoulders, tied my sleeping bag and climbed up dumpsters or drains so I could practice painting words taller than my body on the flat panels, rooftops nobody would ever see.

The boy I found at the empty pool, he painted too. "When you whisper 'olive juice', it looks like you're saying 'I love you,'" he said after he painted it across the floor of a bank's roof. Crooked cursive. As tall as a toddler. I crouched down beside his painted words. He took pictures in the moonlight. Disposable camera. Small flash.

Day zero, before the count down. Dad's family orbited around him, his body bloated like a starfish, sprawled on the hospital bed. The circle of us rotated to stand beside his right ear. Bending down, one at a time, we whispered whatever words sprouted out. When my turn came, I had nothing to say. I sat slumped on the little doctor stool beside Dad's left ear. His bright, brown hair, damp from ear to temple. A bit of blood dried on the lobe. His skin was jaundiced, so swollen I could see the pores. His eyelashes invisible, sucked into the swell of the lids. This person, he will not hear me.

A hand touched the top of my head and a voice said, "Say 'I love you,'" so I said something else and then a whisper, "I love you."

Olive juice.

After I fell against the half pipe, I painted, and little flecks of blue and yellow flew into the torn skin. I could not wash it off.

The boy wanted to have sex. He struck muscle man poses. I laughed until my nose ran, blackish, filled with paint. It looked like dirt. The light was on, and I told the boy I was not ready. We had fucked so many times before, but it had been dark, our hands following each other's bodies, half-dressed, not lit bald, limbs coiled around each other. The boy moved closer. I watched a trail of sweat slip down the side of his neck.

Dad, his hair wet along his ear, a shell, mine bitten. A mouth across the blood on my shoulder. The blood on my ankle when Dad's last dog bit me as I guided Dad's body toward the car, the hospital, the swell. Ankle, shoulder, ear. A breath siphoned into the ear too late to invade that vibrating cave. The ear hears nothing.

How many days?

Dad leaves the ice cave before I can reach him, and I find his ball cap abandoned on the floor. When I pick up the cap, it's the right size for a boy, not a man.

Before the hospital, he'd be fine for weeks, working and playing his guitar. One day he woke up a little yellow. The next day more. The cramps that twirled up his legs burned fierce. He woke up howling, our dogs whining, their bodies wound around his legs.

A few days later, he'd narrow his eyes at the kitchen table like it had gone fluid. Dad rested his hand on the pale oak, fell in, curled over himself as a cramp moved up to his legs toward his abdomen. He reached into the side pocket of his cargo shorts, pulled his keys out, and shook them at me.

Blood twining up through the voices of dogs.

900 days or 300 or 9000. I filled sketchpad after sketchpad with drawings, plans for paint and walls. I recounted the days since Dad had really died. *Where is he?*

Was my counting even correct? Did he die on December 20th or 21st? I found his death certificate, but it was surely lying. The doctor looked at his sparkling wristwatch several hours after the toxins twirled out of Dad's liver, turning off his brain. Was I really only fifteen years old then? Was I really only eighteen years old now?

Impossible.

Am I still (his) child?

My cuticles were filled with plastic colors, paint that never seemed to leave. I lifted my hand to my mouth, breathed in the perfume.

Have I told you that the boy wore ball caps?

Before he died, Dad dripped patchouli over his furniture. The leather love seat and blue, cloth recliner. He shimmied it over the hair of the little dog that bit my ankle the last night he was alive. Patchouli, the smell that brought him back to the days, those dreams, the needles, that virus.

Dad's blood on the grey t-shirt sheets tucked loose along the sides of his thin mattress. His body in the doorway, leaning against mine. We walk toward the car. The little dog, his oiled hair, he jumps off the bed, mouth open. He runs toward my ankle, bites, tries to pull me back.

Don't leave.

The days stretched long and thin. I learned how to drop in.

How many days?

I counted to fall asleep.

I stopped sleeping.

One night, I watched my friends tossing food into each other's mouths and laughed at the little dabs of ketchup hitting their eyelids and necks. One by one, they stopped laughing, but I didn't. The boy laid his hand on my thigh and squeezed a little. I laughed harder. I tried to drink water, but it streamed out of my nose. I tried to stop laughing, to quiet myself down. I covered my mouth with my hands.

Where is he?

I stood up, picked up my board, and left. I skated fast to the tallest hill nearby. I stopped laughing, but my breath came out weird and hard. It was late, no cars out, no bodies skating beside me. I scratched the scar on my ankle.

Itch itch itch, my tag was "itch."

I pointed my board at the bottom of the hill and dropped in.

The summer before Dad died, I took a nighttime photography class. I developed all of Dad's old film, the friends he knew, their needles, mostly dead. He touched the pictures, introduced me to their faces. This one an old girlfriend, her nipples showing through a pale tank top, a hand reaching toward her from the bottom right of the frame. This one all smoke and blurred bodies. This one a shadowed profile, a guy with a beard and a ball cap like Dad's but not quite.

One night after the class ended, Dad picked me up in his boxy Lincoln and drove me to a restaurant for a 2 for $20 steak special. One night, he sat across from me dumping hot sauce on his steak and said, "You know I'm going to die before you finish high school?"

"I know." I cut my steak while he spoke. Small bites.

Dad said, "You have to try find something to do to take your mind off of it, when I die."

"Like art?"

"Something with your body, too. You have to feel it. You used to play soccer, right? Maybe soccer. You have to move."

He chewed, swallowed, "But not drugs, okay?"

Not needles. Not that bite. Not that blood.

I didn't grieve for almost three years. He died, and I counted, but then the dreams came. And the cement. Dropping into it. My shoulders hunched knees bent spine curled belly, my belly a cave.

I kept moving. At night, I filled the alleys between foreclosed businesses with bad graffiti. My tag changed from "itch" to a picture of a sailboat, the kind a little kid would draw. Triangle, stick, and belly.

"Why?" the boy asked. I told him the shapes were simple and soft. The boat everyone wants to ride, but nobody really can. The boat Dad drove at a Florida State Park when I was four years old. The boats Dad drives when I sleep.

The dreams changed. At night, I fell into a swirl. Colors or voices. I felt my teeth clench. Someone sitting on my stomach. Half awake, my body stiff under the weight of him.

I was the last person to see Dad before he seized.

The night before, I drove him to the emergency room, where he was admitted for liver dialysis. His prognosis was six months. I went to a friend's house to sleep. I woke up before dawn, drove back to the hospital. When I arrived, Dad was awake but drugged. Early sun through the blinds, across his face.

He squinted at me. "I'm not going anywhere, yet," he said.

I sat on the edge of his bed. I nodded.

The sun was so bright. I looked down at my feet. I felt the bed bounce. I stood up, and saw Dad's hands shoot up above his head then relax. I backed away from his bed. A hand pulled me by the shoulder, backwards, out of the room.

People in scrubs moved past me, silhouetted by the sharp lines of sunlight. They rushed around Dad's bed. They touched machines and whispered. On the bed, Dad's body curled and straightened. Stiff then soft. Stiff then soft.

The little dog bit me and I kicked him off. A small howl leaked out up from belly deep faded pixels of blood of ink smeared on the side of a milk carton smeared with moving sweat laughing in the ice cave bleeding from the belly sitting sprawled where I slipped on the cement my fingers crawl in I crawl into the cave through the crowd of mouths chewing on failed liver and onions liver and onions that's what Dad ate at the hospital when he was nineteen and drove into dropped into a train but he didn't die then the train kept moving and he kept moving through the crowd in the hospital cafeteria where I drank stale sour tea ten minutes after he seized and his brain died upstairs, I see his hair.

I hear his shoes. I have to crawl faster through the crowd. I have to reach him before his ball cap falls like a feather onto the ice floor and when I get there he's gone of course again, and I touch the ball cap with my hands in my hands. I lift it the canvas ball cap his ball cap my ball cap, everything he left, his ball cap is for a child not a man, too small but stretching, stretching.

I Trust You Can Find It

Mary Miller

I don't like talking about farming, he says, but when I ask him questions he answers them in great detail. He loves farming. He loves getting dirty, being outdoors. He loves coming home at night to eat ice cream and sit on the couch without guilt. I often say the same thing: I don't like talking about writing, but I can talk about it for hours. One thing writing has taught me is that I love to be the center of attention, and when I can't be the center of attention, I would rather be alone.

I meet him at the place he calls 'behind Nissan,' which is miles and miles from the Nissan plant. I follow my GPS instead of his directions, knowing it's a bad idea. It takes me to the right road but I turn the wrong way. I go too far, get lost. I call him, tell him there's a plane on one side, a juke joint on the other. Neither of us can take directions, or give them, and it's the only time we become truly annoyed with each other. I trust that you can find it, we say. And we always do.

I've only come to deliver drinks and a bag of peanut M&M's, but he asks if I want to ride in the combine. Yes, I want to ride in the combine. I have my boots on, a short dress. I haven't showered today.

You need a hand up? he asks. The machine is very tall—I have to climb up five steps—but I don't want a hand up. I want to be able to do everything myself. He is not my husband, but my boyfriend. There was a time when I wasn't even sure he was that. Now he's my boyfriend again but it feels like a trial, every day we are together, every phone call, they are all part of the decision he will have to make about me: will he or won't he? It is a decision I don't care to make either way.

It smells horrible.

Rats made a nest of the cabin, he says. They made babies and ate through the wires.

I sit on a hard bench and it's all so dusty and awful and I don't know how anyone spends so much time in a place like this. He reverses the machine and positions it at the start of a row of dried corn. The corn is ready to be picked when it looks dead.

The combine has big teeth that he navigates between the rows. I want to know how old the machine it is, how much it costs, when the combine was invented. He has no idea when it was invented. He doesn't like to talk about specifics when it comes to money but says they are very expensive, which is why theirs smells like rat piss and breaks down a lot.

He wears a straw hat, no sunglasses. It is a beautiful day, hot, and I watch the machine eat up the stalks and turn them into pieces of corn like so much gold. We're going fast, maybe fifteen miles an hour, it's hard to tell from so high up.

How do you get corn on the cob? I ask. Do you use a combine if you want the whole corn?

He's not sure. He imagines they shuck it. I'm sure there is some other machine for this.

This corn is for pigs, he says. Not for people. It's a wonder, all of this land, all of these people living on all this land, farming it, a way of life I thought had passed.

When the bin is full, his brother pulls a dump truck beside the combine and a great arm swoops out and spews the kernels into a bin.

They bounce and glisten. I want to dive in and throw it all around like Scrooge McDuck, like those bins full of plastic balls I played in as a kid.

After

Ruben Rodriguez

I saw her from across the lawn
her air a blue-green swirl
like soft curls in the constant state
of unfurling. The sound
her flat feet on concrete:
her march, trudging through muck.

It's the time and the sun
the bead of sweat that lingers. I've seen it,
up close, newly formed.
                        Seen the way
two trees will sway towards each other
despite the absence of wind.

She's seen it too. I know, because
she told me, in a whisper held captive
by blurred memory.

I saw her across the lawn
        with a smile—maybe.

Cracking Inside (Main and Sargent)

Alexis Fedorjaczenko

I. There
was yellow police tape strung around one block.

Before that blockage I drove Main Street
every day, learned its patterns well enough

from a car window; darkened bar
bodega and body shop with tenements above.

> ***
>
> i. This Main Street never lived up to our American cliché. Even
> at the start of the city, Main Street was the district that housed
> small hotels of ill repute and itinerant lodging.
> ***

I circled that cordoned block with my car, crawled deeper
into tenement fields, doubled back.

Finally I wondered enough to wander there on the weekend
scanning the street for signs of

constr

destr

obstr

I found none
of the above.

A sign read: Businesses are Open.
I saw one place so far gone

its inside floors were carcass organs
rotted and collapsed, its facade

a strong exoskeleton still.
When I saw sawhorses by a corner tenement

I knew I'd found my trouble

    ***

    ii. In Massachusetts, a tenement house is legally any building
that is rented, leased, or let to be lived in by more than two
families. In common speech it refers to such a building that is
large and run-down or overcrowded.

    ***

a man in an orange vest told me, the building had cracked.

A corner rental whose two street-sides were studded
with bay windows encrusted with classical particulars.
I had long ago fallen for these fabrications

    ***

    iii. In 1880 only two U.S. cities had housing as crowded as
    Holyoke's—Hoboken, NJ, and New York, NY. In that year,
    there was an average of 10.5 persons to each 2-bedroom tene-
    ment apartment in Holyoke. Such was the environment that in-
    dustrial development had created where, decades before, cattle
    had browsed in the open countryside.
    ***

the generosity of the facade seduced me.
I built stories on the little I saw, Christmas strung

in the windows and light falling outward.
Once from my car at night I glimpsed an embrace

thought life was like a movie. This story
collapsed

after most of the children had gone to bed. A knock
on a neighbor's door. The apartments had broken

in half, cracks ran along the floors
and walls. The tenants felt the shake

***

iv. As one urban biographer of the time wrote, "had the devil himself designed these buildings," they could not have been more villainously arranged."

***

bathtubs and toilets fractured
floor slanted down.

***

v. The upper and middle classes were introduced to the tenements via Jacob Riis' bestselling *How the Other Half Lives, Studies among the Tenements of New York* published in 1890. Riis' photos and written journalism about conditions in the tenements shocked the public and resulted in many reforms.

***

After all these years one half of the world
still does not know how the other.

My own awareness is still in the making.
The man in orange threatened danger yet the building looked

***

vi. By 1910, just after the cracked tenement was built, still only New York and Hoboken contained more people per dwelling. Holyoke housed an average of 11.9 and one neighborhood had 22.3 persons for the same amount of space.

***

so still.
The man stood smoking. He and I stared

up at four supposedly unstable stories
saw nothing so I ducked under that police line

to press my face against the front door's glass.
The man shouted

I told him I just wanted to see the weight
under which that building sagged.

II. Nowhere
before had I lived near so much lack.

The mortar between bricks seemed to suck sunshine
out of the sky, heat hallways

sour with slow patience and piss.
So many blocks had burned by then

> ***
>
> vii. The early tenements tended to have only a single room
> that received direct light and air. As a reform, airshafts were
> required and dumbbell apartments, so called for their narrow-
> waist, were built to let dim light in between close buildings.
> ***

the tenements that remained stood spindly
their notched walls too slender

the windowless ones naked
now next to nothing but air.

     ***

     viii. By 1938, 2,800 of Holyoke's dwellings were found to be
     substandard in a survey by the city's new housing authority.
     Around the same time, a newspaper reported that the number
     of vacant tenements was rising. People left the bad ones and
     never came back.

     ***

Once I started looking the collapses piled up.
Another tenement on Main Street shed bricks

onto passerby, another nighttime draining.
Camera crews captured young mothers

in pajamas, the things they carried
never everything. The looters got some

a boy dropped a plasma screen
before he ran. I thought then all the time

about walking out and never coming back
whether I would be glad to go.

I walked Main Street more often then
wondered if the devil himself had designed this destruction

or how exactly things stopped so swift.
Perhaps I could not see where they continued.

Pompeii seemed like a close kind of ceasing
like a building crack suddenly could be coming for so long.

    ***

    ix. There were tenements in Pompeii, too. Records kept in other
    places and therefore not destroyed show that efforts to regulate
    the height and construction of buildings in Pompeii often failed.
    ***

In Pompeii people raised their hands to the gods or they believed
there were no gods any longer

just one last night.
But gods or no gods the world continued

in and out of lightness.
Around the tenement, city life continued too.

Traffic resumed its flow and drivers ceased to slow
and stare, for there was nothing to be seen.

The man in orange had warned against looking
but I kept my eyes drawn up

thought then all the time about what's unseen
on the insides.

III. Here
in the mills, the breaks came first

when business closed
and buildings are falling down in pieces

but still we make home spaces
that stroke against all this decay.

    ***

    x. A mill is technically any building for mechanical trade or manufacture, the term often combined with prefixes to indicate the end product or material (paper mill). During the nineteenth century the image of a mill as a multi-story brick building by a river or canal replaced that of the earlier mill as a small wooden structure on the side of a stream.

    ***

In the old days
immigrants came for these mills and settled

for the rest
crammed and jammed and crowded

into tenement rooms, the lucky ones
traded up.

***

xi. A mill is frequently a large building with a vast number of
windows arranged to throw daylight over all parts of each story.
Early industrial architecture evolved toward a single ideal: ex-
ploitation of natural light and ventilation over maximum span
of space.

***

I live a secret penthouse life now
in this space not meant for shelter

sprawl into more sun-filled space
than can be filled, building

something all our own.
But breaks creep around every street corner

***

xii. In social science, the broken windows theory suggests that
the condition of our physical environment influences our be-
haviors. Dereliction begets dereliction in a kind of irreversible
decline. A broken window might lead to a break and enter. Con-
versely, they say, if a neighborhood is clean, it is more likely to
stay that way.

***

the windows of a building beside my own were rock-cracked
every time they were replaced

until those owners made clear that the only kind of fool
un-boarded

is the kind of fool who lives here.
Even the worst mill builds

***

xiii. Comparative studies find that the broken windows theory holds true; police calls drop in the neighborhoods that are
tidied, graffiti incites theft, and cleaning induces order. Other
studies, and life itself, suggest that the relationship is far more
complex. Critics have shown that the race of residents does more
to influence perceptions of neighborhood crime than any objec-
tive rating of dereliction.

***

do not out-crowd those old tenements
or deliver more dereliction

but some in town see the mill's simplicity as an excess
of undoing, a labyrinth of fire-risk and air sickness

those same neglects back again
in new skin. They call for our eviction.

IV. Everywhere
I look there seems to be deferral.

The owner promised repairs but after the police tape
that tenement was sealed

curtains still curled in open windows
air conditioners still slung above corbels

the center column still failed.
So quickly she had become branded

     ***

     xiv. Abandoned buildings are those determined by the building
     inspector to be deserted with no intention of being reoccupied.
     They are open to the weather. The city places a red "X" on the
     most decayed, so that the firemen know.
     ***

never quite closed up nor torn down, trapped
in transition. I live in-between as well

crave fresh starts but find myself remaining
in this city that other people seem forced to leave.

     ***

     xv. Holyoke's Lyman Terrace was one of the first low-income
     housing sites of the New Deal, a proposed solution to problems
     of the past.

Lyman Terrace was recently the subject of a petition for destruction based on mold, asbestos, indefensible spaces, and years of disrepair. Even the most ardent opponents of demolition concede that major renovations are necessary. But the residents have been fighting to stay.

***

All around there is departure
yet not everyone wishes to go. Many want to stay

put, stay safe, stay the night even
when all these longings

contradict. I think now all the time
about what handcuffs people to their homes.

***

xvi. A 1970s housing report cited 40% of urban Holyoke housing as substandard and diagnosed the tenements as having "a kind of urban arterial sclerosis less the product of age than of heredity."

***

I have lately started to see reversal
that puts me in mind of spring. After too many years

here I have begun to pretend
to move. I shift

possessions around the loft, sorting
as if it mattered just how much there was to carry;

a cleansing ritual more rooted
in self-actualization than safety, the confounded luxury

of the ability to leave. I still look
at blank windows, fix my eyes

on what is seen but probe deeper for the glare
that belies all this decay. The lights come back

in some rooms of the tenement on Main.
I drive by slowly to ensure that brightness

equals life. This is not like a movie now, not nearly
so simple

not even like a novel in which that scarlet letter
would simply fall away.

If a building crack could come
and go as it pleases, so can I.

Epsilon Converses with the Stars

Cameron Schott

Epsilon was cordial to the stars as he drifted among them, exchanging pleasantries with the void as if talking to an old friend. The light of some unnamed sun reflected on his visor and he closed his eyes to bask in the warmth. "Thank you very much," he said to the sun. "That's very kind of you." He made a motion as if he were tipping an imaginary hat to the titanic star.

Darkness took the sun into its hands and Epsilon was once again drifting through the black vacuum. He let out a yawn and, by habit, his hand rose to catch it, though it merely fogged up the glass of his helmet. As he did this, an unusual little particle landed on his finger, and after inspecting it, he realized that he was heading in the direction of a green moon. "Oh, delightful," he quipped, never more genuine. He raised his arm to check his watch. "It's been so long," he said to the stars.

After another hour of cheerful floating, he landed feet-first on the surface of the strange moon. Its surface was blanketed with moss and full of craters. It was small, though; he could see its curvature from where he stood. "Do you mind?" he asked the moon before kneeling down and taking some of the moss in his hand. "I just want to try a piece," he said. "It's been quite some time since I've eaten, and this looks edible enough." He unplugged the feeding tube on his suit and stuffed the moss into it, then with a few more button presses, it was on its way to his mouth. "Ew," he shouted, gagging. "No offense, friend, but this isn't very good at all."

With a foul taste in his mouth, Epsilon walked the moon in search of something new. Eventually, he noticed in the distance a stream of some alien liquid, shining like glass in the starlight. He approached the stream and dipped his hand into it, and the liquid fell like gelatin. "Think I can drink this?" he asked the stars. The silence that followed meant yes, so he put the weird stuff into his feeding tube. It tasted like copper and black licorice. *Why does everything in space taste like copper and black licorice?* Disappointed, he made a great leap and returned to the ebony sky.

"I think," Epsilon said, "that I'd have had a better time at the bottom of the sea." He was spinning through the blackness as he said this, and there followed several seconds of silence. "Don't get me wrong," he added defensively, "I love space and all, but I think I like looking at it more than I like living in it. It's so empty—and dark. It's like a spooky basement that goes on forever."

The silence continued.

"That reminds me, I think Halloween is coming up. It's tough to say of course, but I think it's in a week or so. I've always loved Halloween." A distant star blinked, as if asking to hear more. "I went as an astronaut once," Epsilon continued. "I got more candy than ever that year. I think it's because I told everyone that I wanted to be a spaceman. Old people eat that stuff up."

In the reflection of his visor, Epsilon saw tears on his cheeks. "I can't talk about it anymore," he said to the stars, who seemed to understand.

Hours later, there appeared in the distance a thousand little lights—a star cluster spread wide across the darkness like fireworks over the bay on the Fourth of July. In the vast expanse of empty space, it appeared like a mirage, reminding Epsilon of the hope of morning. He spoke again as it passed by. "Beautiful, wasn't it?" Outer space was quiet and respectful. "Do you want to play a game?"

"I spy with my little eye, something…black. Yes, it's space. I know. Well you're not giving me much to work with." It was like this whenever he and the stars played this game.

"Alright, your turn." Several silent seconds. "Something white? Is it my suit?"

It was. He and the stars were tied. The score was something like 300–300, but who was keeping count. "Maybe we should play the quiet game for a while," suggested Epsilon.

Epsilon felt weak now, going as long as he had without food. He wiggled his fingers to make sure they still worked and was alarmed by how loose his suit had become.

"Why yes," he said, "I have lost weight. Thank you for noticing."

His stomach was growling, and he was on the verge of dehydration with nothing in his midst to give him solace. As his journey wound down, he remembered the life he left on earth, and for a minute, he felt near to it still.

In the distance, a thousand little lights, like fireworks over the bay.

Elegy for Mercury

Meredith Hamilton

You liked to stroke
the travertine of my
collarbones, dip your
fingers in the pools

that formed there
in rain. You said
you loved me best
at the sharpness of my

hips and all the hollow
places. So I held myself
close, pulled my skin
tight over scaffolding

delicate as leaf vein,
then piled my plate
high with spoonfuls
of air I lived on alone

until I disappeared.
Isn't that what you

always wanted?
Hidden by sun,

I'm so small you could
almost miss me.

Rumors the Color of Blood

Oliver Rice

Take this out of history, for the moment.
The hawk, perched on the fence post.

He blinks.

The crisping leaves of the sumac
await the next instant,
the spider web in the thicket,
the creek, the sky,
the killing field.

He blinks.

All of life is brought to bear
on the imperatives of the morning,
the millennia.
On the motion of the light.
The unseen.

He blinks.

Rumors the color of blood,
of mist, of shadow,
whir, click,
rustle through the gama grass,
the stillness.

So it is.
Put it back.

After Han Gan, "Groom with Two Horses"

Ricardo Pau-Llosa

The man behind the blinds watches
the blackbirds eat the bread
and seeds he has scattered richly
on the concrete slab in his yard.

He ponders, the way the bellied groom
in the T'ang painting looks
at neither the white horse he sits on
nor the black one in the foreground which crooks

its head away from us. It leaves an outline
of the muzzle where the painter
figured his stallion would be by now.
Given there is no math to such turn

and jolt as beasts are prone to, and given
the painter projects himself into his work
as the groom, he inverts the yin
of outline and the yang of volume's dark

so, much as the man with his birds,
the painter can also capture gaze

and what he grasps at once. Thus he herds
together the many horses that graze

in the mind and the many who lose
color to become pure form, flat
yet full and moving. Studied rupture, like those
birds, hungry. Dabs against the matte

wet grey that blurs crumbs and presses
leaves into pleats of tunic. The groom's beard
is a coal smudge. In the sudden flight of the present—
the stallion's tail and doves, the dew and the bread.

An Invitation

Cindy King

Night crawlers:

let the feet I stomp at night
in rubber boots above your houses send
you back into the dirt, as deep
in your earth as you may go—
through rock and clay,
crust and mantle,

and then deeper.

Earthworms of so many hearts
and so few brains, empurpled in lust
at midnight, smelling of mushroom
and sprouted potato.

Flee from my tread, peel
yourselves from your lovers. Return
once again to blindness.
Dig down past the roots

and hide
    as you do
from the sun's unforgiving.

    Stay away from the point of my pen,
keep me from pressing you between the dead leaves
of my notebook, as the carnivorous plant
feeds, not to chew,
but to disappear its victim. Keep

this writhing thing, worm that was my husband,
from coming back

to life.

The Couple on the Roof

Jen Knox

Anthony's wrapped knees bent to ease the wobbling. Everything about this simple chore felt complex. His lack of dexterity, the pain, the nagging desire to ease back down the ladder. He examined the tree and adjusted his feet, testing out his equilibrium. But just as he extended the tape measure to the thickest branch—he one that quivered threateningly near the bedroom window during storms—the ladder tilted, skidding along the ceramic-studded asphalt tiles.

It fell as Anthony reached out. He looked over his shoulder in time to make out the blur of his wife's taillights; he waved as she turned the corner with a screech.

His stomach, unaware of circumstance, churned audibly in anticipation of the celery and peanut butter he'd prepared himself as a reward for completing this task. Given all the trouble this was turning out to be, he decided he was due an actual peanut butter sandwich now, complete with lightly toasted nine-grain bread. Hold the celery.

He positioned his feet into a slightly wider stance as the ladder bounced off the bush. The metal taunted him with a clang, landing unevenly, slowly sinking into the pool. He was safe but, alas, stuck on the roof.

Georgia had instructed him, repeatedly, not to go up on the roof because, apparently, she'd known better. He felt a sort of dumb vulnerability as he looked out at the yellow-green grassed and xeriscaped lawns.

Anthony had ignored his wife's warnings because he wanted to prove her wrong, and he knew he could do the job quickly if the branch wasn't too thick. Unfortunately for Anthony, he couldn't use this extra time productively, as the chainsaw was still on the bench by the garage. Georgia would've chuckled at this development.

If she had her way, Anthony would be a fixture in the living room; he'd live for the sole purpose of hauling in groceries and preparing her nightly footbath before *The Voice*—then excusing himself as she watched because, according to her, Anthony chewed too loudly and ruined the show. To make matters worse, as much as Georgia wanted an inert husband, *she* was always on the go. She would be gone today for four hours—the duration of her shift at the craft boutique.

Anthony examined the clouds. Cirrus? Cumulous? Neither seemed quite right for these clouds, which appeared a worn out comforter shielding the sky. He felt like a character in one of those Griswold movies, only there were no endearingly irritating family members holed up in the house to rescue him or even check things out in case he fell. His body, he imagined, would land like a bag of sand on the thorny rose bushes below, or roll into the pool as the ladder had. There was no heroic scene in which he'd dive successfully from roof to pool, especially not with the ladder crossways and slowly sinking.

The hiss and grumble of a motorcycle down the road set Anthony's sandwichless stomach on edge. He had been standing rather securely to this point but now felt the grainy roof tiles sliding along the bottoms of his sneakers. He repositioned his arms around the thick tree branch he'd hoped would be firewood by now, and hugged it tight, then positioned himself like a ballerina, his long and narrow feet creating the V of first position that allowed him to squat some and relieve the pressure on his knees.

Anthony tried to visualize success. He imagined himself flipping off the house, landing like a cat. So many years had passed since he felt any semblance of control over his body, but his mind was elastic—so said his shrink. He felt a rush of adrenaline, then shifted to hear something in his knee pop.

Creaky and watchful, he scanned the perimeter. A neighbor would notice soon enough, he was sure. He saw the man from the Harley out front Josephine's place, hesitating to knock on the front door. It looked like the scene of a romance, the other man almost finally making that move, then backing away.

"Hey," Anthony yelled, but he could barely hear himself, and this guy was a ways down the street. Josephine's husband was no good. The guy was a drunkard, showing up on the front lawn, naked and yelling, running after teenagers who looked at him the wrong way; he'd been seen threatening Josephine in public more than once. Anthony had even caught him pissing in Georgia's rose bushes once at 2 a.m. and had to quietly grumble at the guy, explaining that he should move on before his wife came out with a rifle.

Anthony wondered if he could manage a way to sit and tried hoisting himself onto the branch, but he couldn't get the momentum. He wanted to sit, but the roof was rather steep. The only way to balance would be a foot on either side of the apex, which would mean some uncomfortable sack shifting.

Anthony loosened one hand from the branch to pull up his circulation socks. They were thick black things that felt a little like torture in this triple digit heat. He remembered a time when he thought old men wore thick black socks during summer in some solidary move of rebellion—a fuck you to all the summer fashions and young people with their fast-pumping blood. It wasn't until he turned seventy-three that he realized they were medicinal. Or at least physically helpful. He wondered why they always had to be black though, not a good color for shorts.

A woman with a golden lab shuffled by, looking up briefly, barely registering Anthony before the lab jerked her toward a squirrel. He didn't know the woman, figured her one of the dozen or so who lived in the cheaper housing at the mouth of the neighborhood. Her workout clothes were mismatched, and the way she moved, it appeared her feet hurt. He called out to her.

"Hello," she said, then continued on.

"Hello!" he yelled. She waved again. "No, *help!*—not hello. *Help!*"

The Harley did a U-turn and raged past them, drowning out Anthony's pleas. *No, go back and knock. That husband of hers is no good,* Anthony thought. The dog surged after the bike, dragging its owner along. Anthony recalled himself in fatigues, crawling on the ground like a spider, unafraid of the world. A tough wind, and he imagined falling instead.

The sun was fading the blue paint on the garage door. The sun was fading the grass—which was now almost hay, damp hay. The lawns and bleached pool bottoms in yard after yard seemed a calling card for the bland lives of Anthony's neighbors, most of whom he'd shared beers and Scrabble games with when Georgia was going through her *How to Win Friends and Influence People* stage. She didn't seem to care much anymore, but for a while she had a running list of all the people she'd picked to show up at her funeral. "I want you to keep a list, too, doll," she'd said to Anthony, who knew his odds of outliving her were slim and didn't much care to keep lists of any sort.

It began to rain. Anthony didn't bother to yell after the young lady again as she picked up speed. He'd been stuck on the roof for almost an hour. His skin drank in the soft rain; he thanked the sky. Maybe he could use this time to think. He so rarely had quiet time. He'd read that meditation was something to master, despite pain or awkward positioning, so he tried it but got distracted when he heard thunder.

Four houses down, he saw a little girl who was said to be something of a terror. She'd once jumped into the back of someone's pickup, getting that poor guy in quite a bit of unnecessary trouble—at least, according to neighborhood legend. He'd also heard that she sometimes broke into neighbors' homes just to expose their vulnerabilities, then left notes about how she'd done it and how they should rethink their security systems.

He remembered the girl sneaking extra handfuls of candy when Anthony and Georgia sat out on the porch in their worn skeleton costumes last Halloween. "That little punk!" Georgia said while the girl was still in earshot. They wore the same costumes each year, bought the same candy, but Anthony had made a mental note to get a little extra next year, just in case she came back. She was on the cusp of being too old to trick or treat.

"She's just a kid," he'd argued that night, smiling at the girl when she glanced back, and distracting his wife by offering to refill her rum and coke.

Anthony squat-hovered like a sumo wrestler. He was extra thankful now for the foresight to wrap his knees that morning, but he wished he'd have eaten the celery and peanut butter before he climbed up. He longed for Georgia to come home. And at the same time, he dreaded her return, which would likely come with taunting and ridicule.

The drizzle stopped, and the windy heat felt as though it was coming from a hair dryer. When the gold Cadillac finally turned the corner, he stood. Georgia's low-heeled shoes hit the drive, and he immediately felt the nerves dancing on his chest. He heard her calling his name, watched as she examined the ladder in the back yard. "Oh, Anthony. How sloppy!" she said, unaware of his position above her. She walked around, looked up. "And the damn tree branch is still there. What'd I tell him?" She couldn't see Anthony due to his position and the relative darkness, which camouflaged his leg so that it too looked like a tree branch. She called his name again. Again.

Anthony considered the ridiculous nature of hiding, and he worried all the more about her response. She'd think he was senile. Hell, maybe he was.

"Hey, she's mean, right?" a girl's voice said, a whisper. Anthony almost fell, scrambling to turn around. He saw, on his neighbor's roof, the little terror with the curly hair and round glasses. She wore shiny pants with geometric shapes on them. She wore green shoes and a yellow striped shirt. Had it been daylight, she might have hurt his eyes, maybe even caused a stroke.

"Your parents let you climb?"

"Mom lets me do whatever. Now shhhh. She'll hear you, Mister."

"Anthony."

"Mister Anthony, we need to be quiet or we'll get in trouble."

"How'd you get up there?"

"Crawled up this gate thing."

"The trellis?"

"Yup. Mom calls me a monkey. I can climb anything. Mister Anthony, I don't want you to jump. I always liked you. When we see you at the grocery, you smile at me. *She* doesn't. Not that many people do. Most kids get smiles."

"Sounds like you're working on pretty healthy anxiety disorder there, little one. People probably smile at you all the time, but you're too short so you just don't see them." Anthony's right foot wouldn't move. It was numb to the point of pricked pain, and he still heard Georgia moving around in the house, calling his name. Her voice was faint. "I need to get down from here, kid. You too. You think maybe you can prop that ladder up for me?"

"Oh sure! Watch how fast I can get down!" She rushed to climb down and in doing so her bright sneaker skidded and flew off. The girl stumbled and as her other leg folded beneath her. Anthony watched the tiny body roll off the roof. He gasped, then yelled out.

"Anthony! What in God's name are you doing up there?" Georgia shrieked.

"The girl! That curly-headed girl crawled up on the Harrisons' roof. She just fell. Go get her!" Anthony didn't wait for the logical thing. He didn't ask his wife to pull the ladder up. Instead, he placed his long foot on the gutter and then angled his toes against the concrete bricks below. When he reached the window sill, he jumped, once more a soldier, landing hard on a soft patch of mud. His knee cracked but still seemed to function well enough when he stood. He was elastic.

"What in the hell did you do, Anthony? How do things like this always happen with you? Are you okay? Where is this girl? I didn't hear anything."

"She fell. She has to be here." Anthony looked behind the bushes, ran—for the first time in years—around the neighbor's backyard, lifting the tarp on the pool and wandering around the side.

"Darling, perhaps I should take you in. Maybe you got delirious from being up on that roof. Were you up there the whole time I was gone? You were, weren't you? You were. There's no girl, darling. Come on in. We'll watch some television and you can run me a footbath."

Just as she threw her thick gray hair back and sauntered inside, Anthony heard a whisper. He crouched down and peered into darkness of a cluster of trees behind his neighbor's home. He saw the girl's bright sneakers and moved toward them.

"A monkey, remember," she said, close to the ground as though in combat. "I can do anything." He smiled her way, hoping she'd see.

As Anthony ran the warm water from the tub, he realized that he hadn't finished the job. He grabbed his chainsaw from the garage and positioned the ladder once again. He didn't bother measuring this time, didn't ask permission; he just began to work at it as his wife dozed off watching *The Voice*. His joints ached and screamed. He angled the blade, spun splinters out of the wood. He allowed the branch to fall and watched it plunk against the bushes. He returned inside, wife none the wiser, and chewed his peanut butter sandwich loudly, unabashedly, as Georgia watched her shows.

"Can you chew quieter? Good-ness!" she said, waking from beneath a light blanket. She waited for a commercial, then turned off the jets in her footbath, removed two wrinkly feet and placed them on a towel gently, then spoke again. "That girl is no good, whoever she is. If you really did see her. We might want to make an appointment at a therapist. We can call the VA."

"Georgia, I don't—"

"Hush. It's coming back on."

Anthony excused himself, walked out the door as Georgia's feet dried, and he dumped the foot water on their struggling grass then upturned the bath and left it on the porch. He felt the ground beneath him, soggy but solid. Anthony's feet had always been particularly long and narrow, tough to find shoes for, not ideal for dancing or balancing. But he used them that night.

He walked along the street, moving until all the stiffness in his joints and ankles eased. He walked until the leaden feeling of his legs dissolved. He knew his wife was dozing again because she wasn't calling after him.

When Anthony's dreams terrorized him, Georgia would cradle his head. She'd stay up all night, stroking his arm from the shoulder, lightly; her touch like soft rain. He never opened his eyes, never let her see his appreciation. When he was wide awake the next day, he wouldn't think of night. She'd gripe about this and that, he'd disagree inaudibly.

The day Anthony spent on the roof, the day he walked for hours into the night, he slept sound for the first time in twenty years. In his dream, he saw the man he'd once been and he ventured toward him, as usual. But then a Harley rushed beside him, and he gave its driver a head nod. A little girl in loud clothes danced on the sky—totally free. People moved all around him, and he smiled at them.

He began climbing onto his roof occasionally after that day, if only to test his equilibrium here and there and get a touch closer to the sun. He began climbing onto the roof daily after a while. He ran footbaths and left the wife to her shows. He kept his eyes closed as the pads of her fingers traced the base of his neck some nights—when the nightmares surfaced.

Then the day came when he tried to sneak out, and she whisper-growled, "And just where do you think you're going?"

No one thing is all one way, Anthony said, positioning the ladder that night. He held it tight, eased up after Georgia, ready in case she decided to back out. But Georgia went along, climbing in her pale green nightgown.

She wobbled on the roof at first, but scanned the neighborhood with intense interest, quiet appreciation. She said she remembered crawling out on her own roof as a girl, leaning back on her elbows and staring up at the sky with her sister, freestyle futures formulating on their tongues.

From their perch, the couple's view stretched out to eternity; Anthony and Georgia's fingers threaded and gazes widened. The girl with curly hair sometimes biked by and waved without looking up. Others expressed concern, asked if the couple needed help. Some whispered that they must be insane.

"Just two old birds who found their perch," Anthony would say whenever people appeared worried. It became their daily rendezvous, no matter what.

Much would remain the same: Anthony would continue to have nightmares on occasion, the imprint of events too deep a wrinkle in his brain to fully erase, but Georgia would continue to cradle his head.

They would continue to bicker and gripe, or offer passive-aggressive silences in exchange for sour words. Anthony would continue to run footbaths and Georgia would watch *The Voice*.

But they'd always return to the roof, where they were briefly a piece of the sky. They would sit there until the time came to fly away.

Last Letter

Ruth Foley

For years, I thought all was forgiveness—
find a way to bless the anger and the roil

and allow myself salvage. But I could
learn only to love your wrists and the skin,

its culpability. I could love the bandages and
thread more easily, true. Dear Turquoise,

you are more than two years dead and more
than twenty trying to die—I wonder if you thought

at last when you were told. I wonder if
the tumors spoke some truth you couldn't hold.

I can learn to love the alcohol, the blade,
the practice runs you asked us all to make.

I loved the desolate calm on the phone from
whatever ward they held you on, you emptied

of everything but sedatives. I can love your refusal
to call me home. I can love the places where

your voice should be. Let's make a pact: you learn
to love the bells I couldn't ring, the mourning prayer

I couldn't begin to write so soon. Learn to love
my jealous grief and my miserly expression. Love

the months I sat inert and silent after I knew,
and love the sounding depths of my abandonment

of you, and I will love the times you failed to die,
the ways you taught me to believe there was

this one thing you could not accomplish, maybe
one thing you had decided you would not do after all.

Training Fire

Adam Tavel

My father parked his Thunderbird in weeds
so high they grazed my underarms. The house,
pitiful and drooped, looked as if a meteor
had plummeted from the distant hand of God
to splinter through its roof and smolder down
into the basement. Its windows blown, the drapes
were a hideous grape and motionless
in August heat. As we crossed the road

I saw his fire company slurping beers
they pulled from coolers nestled in the shade
beneath the running board on their water truck.
I didn't turn to look when pick-ups whooshed
and made a little breeze that billowed through
my Captain Planet tank-top. The chief,
with shrapnel scars whiskerless and pink
inside his bristle-beard, limped across the yard

on his prosthetic leg to share a Sprite,
tussle my bangs, and plop his helmet on
my head. No sound passed its padded flaps.
Its visor's greasy veil of glass transformed

cornstalks wilted brown from the nearby field
into a jagged blur. Flush-faced, I flipped
it up and saw the smoke start chugging out
like blackened waterfalls reversed.

The tiny hairs across my forearms baked
until I retreated to the ditch's cloud
of flies that stormed above its stagnant muck.
The men, unmoved, stood sweating through their jeans
so bad their denim backsides were two shades
darker than their thighs. Their cigarettes
waggled as they laughed, dangling from lips
that drew and blew to help blot out the sky.

It was then, a flash, a hand, a girl's
that for an instant I thought peeked out
to sway the drapes, though later I was told it was
the draft and nothing more. I imagined
she ran to hide inside her mother's closet,
a knapsack of seashells in her arms,
overlooked on the final sweep before
an angry match awoke and bloomed its rage.

Cowering she sobbed, dazed and trapped inside,
her ankle caught between a floorboard's gash
as rafters fell, as embers singed a sundress
her older sister stitched from fabric scraps
she found one night while rummaging a mouse
that scampered through the attic's cluttered piles,

a mouse she sought to shoebox for a pet.
She was calling out as loosened bricks

shivered from the chimney, as the second story
slacked and smashed all around her body's curl.
Her bestial wail bellowed through the roof
no longer roof at all—impotent, raw,
merciless as a crow-caw, my whole mind
swallowed whole by her shrieking mouth
until I felt the strained constricting throb
inside my throat and knew the scream was mine.

Baptism

Matthew Robinson

The sun shone white against the chow hall trailer, lighting the day but bringing no heat. Sunday breakfast. Most of the battalion sat warm inside. At the round plastic picnic table out back, Mills, Mason, and Doc watched their breath between bites. "Security is way better than missions," Mason said, dragging a sausage link through syrup. "All the down time. All the phone center. Internet café. All the breakfast."

"Fuck that," said Doc. "Time crawls on FOB security. Give me mission rotation any day. It may not be fun work, but it fucking goes." He mashed his eggs with the tines of his fork until they were the consistency of hummus.

"I like the hotels," Mills said. "No brass. Sheets on the beds. It's almost like not being here." He began cracking up the shells of his hardboiled eggs.

Mason leaned in over his paper bowl of oatmeal, struggled to dissolve a particularly difficult sugar clump, pressing with the round back of his spoon.

"You waited too long," Mills said. "It's too cold. Pour in a little hot coffee."

Mason dribbled his coffee and smiled at the resulting melt. "How was the week? I heard there was some shit."

"Who are you asking?" Doc said, scooping scrambled eggs onto toast.

"You," Mason said. "Mills is in my platoon, I know how his week went. Besides, he's an NCO—he's doing *just* fine."

"Here we go," Mills said.

"Doesn't share a room, doesn't have to pull TOC duty, doesn't have to clean the shitters—I can keep going."

"Of course you can. You can bitch all fucking day, except those shitters aren't going to clean themselves."

"Ha-ha," Mason said. "Eat a dick."

Doc took a big bite of breakfast. "Actually, something did happen." He swallowed. "I am now in the soul-saving business."

"How's that?" Mills said, pressing the whites of his eggs into salt.

"A couple of Joes in my platoon have been all worked up about this being the holy land and all. Said it's too badass to be here as Christians and not do anything about it. So get this…" Doc bit hugely into egg-slathered toast. "They talk Sergeant Cortez into taking the Chaplain out to the Tigris and fucking baptizing them. I didn't even know. We roll out for what I thought was a goddamn combat patrol and as soon as we get to the river we pull over and out jumps the Chaplain and these two guys start stripping off all their gear and wading into the fucking water. And let me tell you, that water is no joke. The land may be holy but that river is *all* shit."

Mason sipped his coffee and swished it across his teeth. Mills bit through soft white, into firm yellow, salt striking tongue.

"And then," Doc said, "just as the Chaplain is dunking the second guy, the first one already soaked to the bone, guess what floats by, barely out of the mud?"

"No idea," Mills said.

"Dead goat," Mason said.

"Better," Doc said, "dead fucking Hajji. Face up and everything, floated by close enough to touch, slow as anything, in no fucking hurry. But you should have seen the Chaplain scurry up the bank." Doc laughed hard, egg left his mouth. "And those sorry, saved, sad-sacks, trudging back to their gear, talking about probably needing shots." He drank orange juice deeply until the straw made sucking noises in the bottom of his carton.

"What did you do with it?" Mills said.

"With what?" Doc scraped his plate clean of egg remnants with his last piece of toasted crust.

"With the body," Mason said.

"What do you mean what did we do with it? We didn't fucking shoot it—we left it." He ate his last bite of breakfast. "We charlie-miked. Drove around for a few more hours, stopped at the hotels and had lunch, then came home. I'll tell you what though, one of those hotels got themselves a George Forman kind of grill and they're making melty sandwiches now. You got to get over there and get one before they figure out we like them and stop making them. So goddamn good."

Mills sipped his coffee, watched the steam rise off and go. "You had a busier week than us." In his plate sat crushed shell, yolk and salt.

Mason held his cup in both hands, thumbed its lip with increasing pressure, until it made a quiet *thunk, thunk, thunk.*

"The night before," Doc said, "we ran into some shit, some sort of celebration over a soccer win or something. Anyway, folks were drinking, enjoying themselves, and of course the shit-heads can't have that, so they started shooting up the crowd. Really brought down the mood." He pulled the straw out of his juice box, stabbed it into a chocolate milk. Began to suck. Swallowed. "We heard the shots from where we were patrolling, it was like two blocks away. We rolled up and fucking laid waste. The crowd had mostly left anyway, the shit-heads were just standing there blasting away with their AK's as everyone ran off screaming. And I'm up on the SAW, stoked to see my first fucking bad guy, you know? And I line it up and *Zip*—shit-head down. *Zip*—shit-head down. Felled them like they were made of balsa. We start taking fire but I'd already cut down half of them. *Zip. Zip.* I get now why that gun is called a fucking SAW. Inside of a minute we're just looking at an empty lot—nothing standing."

Doc's straw sucked air again. He piled his bowl, napkins, utensils, and empty drink cartons onto his plate. Took them to the trashcans. He stood looking into the black of the garbage bags. Mills and Mason finished their coffee and gathered up their plates and bowls.

"You shoot up shit all the time," Mills said. "What do you mean those were the first enemy you've seen?" He slung his rifle across his chest, squeezed the handgrip until the diamond pattern left an itching sensation in his palm.

"Well, I mean I shoot back when we take fire, but it's like they're invisible, I can never make them out. I just shoot at where I think the bullets are coming from. Or if something explodes, I just shoot across my entire sector of fire. But it's never an actual person looking back. This was the first time they were just standing there, you know? It's always so fucking spooky. It finally felt right."

As they walked towards the motor pool the sun shone yellow across the FOB, lighting the day but bringing no heat.

When to Say *Uncle*

Paulann Petersen

—*for Richard Theobald, my mother's brother*

Tell me about the war. Not mortuary school before you enlisted,
not opening that key vein in the neck, blood running out easy, fast
into a stainless steel pan. Enough about the makeup to make
a wife sigh, *Nice, he looks peaceful, like he's only asleep.*
An illusion to fool grief. Not that. No tricks.
For now, put your white hankie
back into your pocket.
                    Tell me about being an Army medic,
with Nana at home stateside, content, believing that you—
her only son—wouldn't be sent to the front lines.
But you were. There first to bring in supplies, you once ducked
behind the crates while a shimmy from Japanese machine guns
shredded bundles of bandages. Saved by a materiel
of mercy. Home from the war, handkerchief out,
you'd make a knot, another knot, a twist,
and a white mouse ran up and down your arm.
I shrieked, laughed, watching its cotton ears
twitch and wave.
                    Tatters of gauze must have littered
the New Guinea mud around those shot-up crates that day.

How many buddies did you later bandage,
wrapping white around a limb, pressing soft squares
onto a groaning chest? How much red throbbed out—
fast, easy—before you could? Bandages are always white.
For a while. Did those GIs look peaceful
once they died?

> I never got to see the professional tricks
you bought and learned, secrets only real magicians knew—
just the hankie-mouse, a stunt to entertain kids. Each time
I saw you, I begged for it. After the war, you abandoned
being a mortician. *Too much death*, you said.
Enough is enough.

> Once you were making your living
calling on physicians—leaving your salesman's trail
of patter and jokes along with samples of your company's
miracle drugs—did you charm those doctors into prescribing
your brand? Could you convince them to scrawl
its name onto a square of white paper—their handwriting
a life-saving sleight of hand?

> The flags for truce
are always white. Only it will do for such waving.
Tell me about the wages of war. Could enough ever be
enough? Talk to me about the bales of gauze, bullet-cut
into bits. Torn, adrift. Tell me you recall South Pacific wind
scattering those suddenly useless bandages,
countless shreds blown along a jeep-rutted road—
all those tiny

> white flags, waving.

somewhere

Toni Hanner

Somewhere a hospital / my mother / i can't find / the number / all plumbers and pizza / dusty floor / bicycle tires split and flapping / sidewalks covered in flowers / the train through illinois / she's dying / where is her white face her hair spread / the pillow / everyone behaves according / to protocol

> i lay in bed watching a small heart pump
> in my upturned wrist

Vox Animalia

after Zanesville, Ohio, 2011

M.K. Foster

My father has fallen asleep again in the living room, fallen
into another dream about *animal*: his father descending into the Pacific
to free an anchor, his father drilling a well through twenty feet of
     bedrock,
his father sawing off the barrel of a shotgun, soldering on a pistol grip.
     Good
for putting down a sick dog or a broken horse. Good for swallowing
     until

the metal tip grates the back of the throat: the muscle twitches as he
     pulls the trigger,
only manages to blast away the jawbone, part of the skull. Pulls again,
     collapses
into a heap of meat on their garage floor. In the dark, my father names
     all his animals,
his mouth moving as though approximating distance, as though
     eating—he, sunk
into the couch again, says *I'm afraid of what I can't control. And I'm
     afraid.* In his dreams,

my father, the body and the body that buries the body: things he
    doesn't say when

he makes jokes under his breath about sucking a bullet like an after-
    dinner mint, eating

a bullet, jokes about grave-making as he arranges flagstones on the
    front walk. *Put them*

down deep enough, dig until you hit ice or water or rock. You don't
    want the neighbor's dog

turning up a hand or some shit like that. I wish I knew how to ask him
    what his dreams

dig up and drop at the foot of his bed: his father, the storm at the
    window and the animal

just visible on the other side of the window. Memory is only domesti-
    cated madness,

I think. Caged and sedated. What becomes of us when we share our
    dreams with

those of the dead? What hungers claim us after our ghosts have
    swallowed us whole?

Beneath the storm, my father's body tenses, folds itself inward, his
    dark shape

piled onto the couch. *Don't touch him*, my mother warns. *He's*
    sleeping. Watching him

from the doorway, afraid to turn out the light, I see the field I saw once
    in a book about

life on earth: in Ohio, a field of animals—tigers, bears, wolves, lions—
    dead in wet clay,

shot after being set free. In the photo, they look like they're sleeping.
     They're a portrait
of the end of the world, their bodies turning the ground into a mosaic
     of Eden. *This is*

why we don't cage a wild heart, the photo says, and *this is why we
     have cages at all.*
Mouth open, breath ajar. My father, the animal and the animal that
     buries
the animal. He breathes in, breathes out. Then, he breathes in, not out.
     He holds
still—something that happens, perhaps, when dream gets in, but can't
     escape. Then,
exhales. *Father,* I want to tell him, *I would have opened the cages for
     all those animals*

*that day. I would have let them run. Father, after we have lined our
     bodies with raw meats*
*and after we have raised the gun to our mouths, after we have pulled
     the trigger, memory is*
*the last to get out, the only animal we can never, otherwise, release.
     Father, do you think God*
will put us down deep enough when we die? In the dark, his hands
     reach up for his mouth:
he is either trying to push the barrel away or trying not to miss what
     he aims for.

shelter, cover

1. to shelter

Impermanence

Kristy Athens

> *You might as well expect all rivers to run backward as that*
> *any man who was born a free man should be contented*
> *penned up and denied liberty to go where he pleases.*
> —Hin-mah-too-yah-lat-kekt

I was recently introduced to the concept of the "First Foods": Water, Salmon, Deer, Cous, and Huckleberry. I live in Wallowa County, Oregon, former home of the Nimiipuu, or Wallowa Band of the Nez Perce Tribe. While actual Nimiipuu were exiled long enough that they are practically nonexistent here as permanent residents, a number of tributes to them dot the valley: a bronze statue of Hin-mah-too-yah-lat-kekt, or Chief Joseph; his father's grave; a small interpretive center; a powwow grounds. Native Americans are given a brief moment of consideration at the beginning of the Chief Joseph Rodeo. One European-American, Alvin Josephy, worked during the twentieth century to preserve the history of the Nez Perce. Another, Rich Wandschneider, works to preserve Alvin Josephy's legacy and also to keep the twenty-first century tribe part of the community—inviting people like Wenix Red Elk to speak at the Josephy Center for Arts and Culture, in the town of Joseph, on a cold day in November 2014.

Winter came early to Northeast Oregon last year. First snow: November ninth. In Wallowa County it can snow any month at all, but in 2014 the Earth ignored a certain time-honored protocol. There was no rain and then cold rain and then sleet-glazing-fenceposts, making everyone wish it would *just snow*.

The wind had kicked in a few days prior. Whenever the wind kicks in around here, you know something drastically different is coming. Before I even had a chance to encase my windows in plastic and dig my warmest boots and long underwear from the storage room in the basement, the temperature dropped to single digits. I arranged for a man named Archie, from the local farmers' co-op, to come up the hill and fill the propane tank.

"Going to be a long winter," we nodded to each other.

My husband and I don't own that propane tank; we don't belong on this land. It is not ours—not the way *no land is anyone's*, the way the land was before the European-Americans took over with their roads and towns and politely reverent monuments. It is not-ours in the sense that we rent a house in the middle of an oat field that is leased to a farmer, Kurt, who lives across the valley, by a couple who moved to Bend to be near their grandchildren. The previous spring, we watched Kurt's circus-parade assembly of spray-tanker, tractor, seed drill slowly work its way around the field. We watched the sprouts emerge and reach for the sun, trying to outpace their clones. We watched the seed heads appear and grow, a few revealing themselves to be wheat interlopers from the previous year. We waved to the "hired hands," a young couple named Bambi and Josh, who buzzed around the field on their four-wheeler to move the water lines. We watched the plants fade from green to gold, dry and harden. We waved at Kurt when he came to check on the stalks in the hot sun, biting a few kernels in his teeth to test their density, wanting the oats as dry as possible without shattering. We watched his harvester cut wide swaths through the field when it was time, grain spewing into a truck, then another truck, then another. Into the night, headlights illuminated the falling grain. Then, Kurt and his machinery were gone for the season, leaving the quiet field to us and our dogs.

My husband and I used to own land; in our mid-30s we bought a handful of acres in the Columbia River Gorge. We thought it would be our final destination. After moving from the Midwest to the Pacific Northwest, and then from house to house in Portland, we were ready to put the proverbial root down. Make a home. Make a life. We expanded the small vegetable garden; converted milking stalls in the barn into chicken housing; hauled fallen trees from our woodlot and built a gazebo. I learned to can and bake. We had a different dog then, and we intended to start a family there.

Within a period of a few years, we had to carry that dog off the road and bury her, and we learned, expensively and painfully, that we were not in fact going to start a family. Reeling from these experiences and from the flagging economy, we lost momentum and had to sell our land. Our place. Our identity.

Two weeks after Wallowa County's early first snow in 2014, winter waned. Thawed out. After Wenix Red Elk drove over to the Josephy Center from the Confederated Tribes of the Umatilla Indian Reservation to talk about the First Foods, the air stilled and the roads cleared. The golden oat stubble that surrounded my house re-revealed itself, only slightly less robust than it had been. The overcast sky broke and the warm sun shone on the still-white peaks of the Wallowas beyond the field, on Chief Joseph Mountain, on my dogs and on me, face upturned. I swear I heard a robin sing and caught a whiff of lilac.

And then, the wind blew and brought winter back.

Near our home in the Gorge were the Bonneville and The Dalles dams. These and other dams tamed the unpredictable, raging Columbia River. The water that backed up eight miles from the The Dalles dam in 1957—that in fact ran backward—buried an age-old fishing site, Celilo Falls. In 1957, ten thousand people gathered on the bluffs above the falls, one for each year that Native Americans had been fishing there. Some believed that the Great Spirit would never allow the falls to be taken away, and came to watch the White Man be foiled by a higher power. A few hours later, Celilo Falls disappeared under the surface of the newly christened Celilo Lake.

Walking across the snowy oatfield and along the ditch that bisects it, I'm able to see some of the things that the dogs sense with their noses on any walk, snow or no snow. Mouse trails, and the little holes the mice make when they hop-hop-hop through the snow instead of running on the ground. The small heart-shapes of deer feet. The bigger elk feet. Pheasant tracks. The dogs run from one to the next, gathering information: species, trajectory, freshness. Who knows what? All I know is that it's serious business. They don't seem to notice the cold. I hunker down into my jacket and wish I'd donned that long underwear.

If the Nez Perce were with me on this hill, they would roll their eyes and say, "What are you doing here? Go down to Imnaha, dummy." At four thousand feet in elevation, the Wallowa Valley was their *summer* home. In winter, they traveled down to the warmer canyons around the Imnaha and Snake rivers, where they lived off the food they had harvested up top.

European-Americans like to think in terms of permanence. They build houses "to last." They like to crisscross the land with fences to hold some things in and keep other things out, and they like to own things, and "pass them on" to their children. Their things. Instead of letting the climate determine their schedule they hunker down and fight it, burningburningburning—wood, gas, oil, coal—to keep warm. Driving their cars on ice to get to the store, to school. Shipping mangos and grapes thousands of miles from the global south.

One day in November, the snow was the texture of an old fleece jacket. It crunched dully, lacking the squeak of fresh, dry powder. Fog had been rolling up and down the valley, flowing from the north like the tide in an estuary. Sometimes we were in the fog, on this slope, and sometimes it roiled below us like a grey, ephemeral sea. Sometimes this transition took just a few minutes; I could stand in the field above the barn and watch it disappear and reappear. Because of the temperature the fog coated everything—every strand of barbed wire, every pine needle—in a white frost jacket. When the sun peeked through, it colored everything in shades of peach and pink. The Nez Perce missed out on this, all warm and cozy down on the Imnaha!

Native Americans don't eat just four things: each food name represents a type of food. Lamprey and other aquatic creatures count as "salmon." All large eatin'-mammals—elk, bison, mountain sheep—are "deer." "Cous" (*coosh*) means biscuit root and other foraged plants. "Huckleberries" includes chokecherries. The groups don't represent just food but also ceremony, and lifestyle; they dictate the migration from one area to the next. Like Farmer Kurt watches the oats, the elder women watch the camas. The elder men monitor the salmon. European-Americans' fences have mucked up tribal migration, but the gathering continues.

The Nez Perce worked the land carefully, moving from one area to another in order to mitigate their impact and follow the peak seasons of each crop. They burned their huckleberry stands in the fall to stimulate new growth in the spring. By living in a constant state of impermanence they cultivated a reliable, renewable cycle. They use the First Foods as the basis for their forestry and fisheries management. They use the First Foods as the basis for their customs. For their identity. Renewal is the closest thing they, or anyone, has to permanence.

Before my husband and I owned our land in the Gorge, a Canadian windsurfer acquired it from a veterinarian, who cut down the prize rhododendrons the previous owner had planted because her goats ate some and died. The house was built in the 1930s in a rare subdivision called Fruit Home Colony in honor of the orchard it was displacing. Before that, of course, it was simply the route from the huckleberries on Pahto to the salmon in Nchi'wana, Big River.

Middle age has brought me to appreciate impermanence. It used to scare me, the idea that, one day, there would no longer be a trace of me in this world. But the wind kicked in at midlife, blowing away the dramas of young adulthood. These days, I find comfort in the idea that none of this will last. None of it, not the way we know it. The cliffs of Celilo sleep beneath the surface of the Columbia. Waiting. The dams will not last forever. A great wind may blow through the Wallowa Valley itself, bringing its original inhabitants to reclaim it.

I plan to hold up my end of the deal and be an active participant in the world, but I have released myself from the pressure and hubris of pursuing permanence. Like camas or Coho, I will live and then I will die. When I do, share my things among you. Tell stories about me. Spread my ashes on the huckleberry bushes and the river.

The Fall

Robert Nazarene

It was a terrible one. The cliff ledge and a billion years
of chiseling rains, misbehaving beneath your boots.
You never felt the crumpling landing—only

the eye-blinding burst of God. Your dog has found
its way down to you and lays its head upon your
shoulder. A picture of desire and its absence.

And your companion—knowing
yet not knowing—your years of faithful friendship
have come to this. Just another one of life's

precipitous ledges. And, save for the dog's
quiet whimpers, sent by God—*all is still.*
And you?

Just another trinket in life's unlucky box
of broken souvenirs. The one named: *Me.*

Spin

Stacey Allen Mills

I.2

That's how I was abandoned or at least how I imagine it went. To be honest, I don't really know. I hope it was something like that—something terribly gritty making my current existence seem more… more… OK I don't know… just more. I've always wanted to be more. My current white, married, white picket fence, 2.5 kids, black labrador retriever with matching minivan life in the suburbs could not be more boring. I'm so bored, I'm not even sure porn is good anymore.

1.3

Quietly Henry closes up his keyboard to walk away. The story seems so different from the last time he wrote it, rewriting it again, and again, and again, always trying to create an alternative ending that provides Henry with more. In truth, Henry is not married, does not have 2.5 children, a minivan, or a white picket fence. Henry does not believe the inferior class should breed—he should not breed—his parents should not have done it, breeding that is. Like so many evenings before, turning off the light, he moves quickly to the elevator. This evening is different. This will be Henry's last evening in the office…his last evening at the keyboard… his last evening of trying to be more. No—this is a lie—Henry will always need to be more. Life has been hard on Henry, threatening to drown him out slowly over the course of time, day-by-day, unmet expectation by unmet expectation; Henry is being drowned out, clearly out. He wants more. He has always wanted more, but it has never come until one day it arrived in the form of a check, an inheritance from his father's estate accompanied by a small box containing his father's wristwatch. Henry has never known his father. The summary of his father's years leading up to this moment in the exposition of Henry's life are a mystery to him, his grandmother—who raised him—never telling him much of his father. Henry cashes the check thinking it will bounce. Oddly, and much to Henry's surprise, the check does not bounce—the funds now sitting available in his account. Just as odd is the curiosity continually sitting within Henry's soul since childhood, the curiosity of not knowing about his father having bubbled up many times over the years between adolescence and adulthood; each new grand release of curiosity forming a different fantasy inside Henry, increasing desire, each new story helping him feel more, want more, want to be more. He paces. He waits. He releases. He waits. He releases. He leaves.

Standing by the gravesite, Henry notices the simplicity of the headstone that only includes his father's name, birth and death date: Calvin Henry Austin 1950–2003. Henry remains stone-faced; the new awareness that he shares a part of his name with his father matriculates around his brain for meaning. Did Henry's father go by Henry or Calvin? He finds no emotion regarding their shared names; the question settles at the bottom of Henry's soul like a rock tossed into a dry riverbed. Henry wonders who chose the headstone? Was it expensive? Did they care? Henry wished the headstone would have included a oneline phrase, "loving father buried here," even though he knew in his heart it would be a lie. Henry could live with a lie, if it were that lie. Henry could lie to himself all day long until he finally believed it, felt comfort in it.

The day is sunny. Rolling green pastoral hills of the cemetery are providing a quiet moment of stillness. Henry appreciates the strong, mature, green trees dotting the property. The cemetery is peaceful, although the undercurrent in Henry's soul winds and unwinds like a child finishing a tantrum; continually fixating on the truth of the situation, he wishes even harder for the lie. Visiting his father's grave is not the "more" Henry is seeking. This is a gravestone placed as a marker of a person he did not know. In this moment, Henry could not feel more less.

2.1

—   I   don't   want   you.

—   Fuck   you.

—   No,   I   really   don't   want   you.

—   Fuck   you.

—   You're   not   hearing   me.   I   don't   want   you.

—

—   I   said,   I   don't   want   you.

—

—   I   said—

—   I   heard   you   the   first   time.

2.2

Today I sit in a coffee shop and read. In walks a white, mid-thirties, middle income, single male, cradling his infant child in his left arm. He orders a to-go breakfast sandwich and a banana. Waiting for the sandwich, he stuffs little broken-off pieces of banana into his son's mouth and licks his own fingers clean. Licking, sucking, wanting, feeding, the child needs safety. The father stuffs little pieces of broken-off banana into his own mouth and licks his own fingers clean. Desiring, fantasizing, touching, sexualizing, the adult male needs connection. The result of these connections have produced this child. The father repeats this practice several times, his dexterous fingers working the one-handed banana dance. I am mesmerized at how calm and how contented the baby presents. I am stunned by the father's ability to engender continual feelings of safety within the child and within himself. The child is safe. The child feels the safety of his father's arms. The child is loved. The child in connected. I'm not sure if I'm looking at the father or the child anymore. The person behind the counter delivers the to-go breakfast sandwich and they leave the coffee shop.

2.3

The house is old, but Henry is visiting anyway. He is invited to enter; an old woman boring him with tea seems a small price to pay for sleuthing. Henry takes in the room as she asks if he wants to let. The previous boarder passed not long ago. "He never kept much stuff," she says, "just a jacket, writing pad, and a book," all of which she has donated to the resale shop on Canal Street. When recounting the list of his father's final possessions, she fails to mention the type-written letter found on the bureau after his death or the wristwatch. The omission is not a problem for Henry, the wristwatch having been placed on his wrist and the letter in his right jacket pocket since the day he received them. She does not know Henry from any other person inquiring to let, which suites him just fine. She assures Henry that the room has been thoroughly cleaned since the last tenant. Henry asks for a moment alone in the room to consider the idea of letting. Sitting on the bed, Henry waits to feel something. The amount of time seems uncomfortable to the old women who is now waiting downstairs in the parlor. He sits on the bed. He waits. No release. He sits on the bed. He waits. No release. He leaves.

3.1

—   I'm   not   more.

—You're   not   more.

—   I'm   not   more.

—   You're   not   more.

—   I'm   more.

—   No   you're   not.

—   I'm   more.

—   Really?

—   Yes.

—   How?

—   Fuck!

3.2

Today is the day I know it will happen. Today is the day... I'm waiting, I'm hoping, I know today is the day Daddy will take me to the store to pick out a new red Schwinn bike just like the one Charlie Hinkle got last year. Today is the day—I will be more. Grandma says Daddy is not coming; I know he is. Today, I'm six.

3.3

Henry acquires his father's jacket, writing pad, and book from the resale shop on Canal Street. Henry buys a new pair of shoes, but he does not know why. Henry places his old shoes in the dumpster. Henry cannot remember the last time he replaced his shoes. Henry wonders if these are the types of shoes his father would have worn. Using the newly acquired shoebox, Henry carefully packs the collected possessions with care. Henry walks to the bus terminal on the other side of town. The new shoes are uncomfortable. He wonders if they will ever feel like his old shoes. Purchasing a ticket, Henry boards the Greyhound bus for an unknown destination. Henry does not know where he will go or which stop will conclude his journey. Each passing mile, each new town, and each dimly-lit bus terminal seems the same to Henry; they all seem the same, they are not more, and he does not disembark from the bus. Eventually he is evicted from the bus in Seattle.

4.1

—	It's	never	gonna	happen.
—		It'll		happen.
—	It's	never	gonna	happen.
—		You're		right.
—		I'm		right.
—		You're		right.
—				What?
—	Damn	right,	it's	never	gonna	happen.
—				Release
—				

4.2

Cheery happy moments, birthday cake, bubble gum, peach cream icing, a white two-layer cake covered in candles, a surprise at the bottom—that is how I imagine it will go. Grandma, green and gold shag carpet that smells like the dog, an extra scoop of ice cream on my best day—I imagine that too. Bounding on the lawn playing catch with Dad, his hands big and strong holding onto me and the ball at the same time. I am eight.

4·3

The record player is currently spinning original vinyl in the Throwback Seattle Coffee Shop. Henry works here one shift per weekend to continually spin "I Got a Name," a song by Jim Croce. The original vinyl sounds more real to Henry than today's modern digital music streams. Admittedly, Henry loves this environment. Today, the Gordon Lightfoot or Simon and Garfunkel songs Henry is spinning at the Throwback Seattle Coffee Shop are either making him weary, nostalgic, or sad; to Henry's surprise, he can feel a multiplicity of diverse emotions all in the same present moment of creation. Yesterday—one of Henry's more hopeful days—he spun "Budapest" by George Ezra. Today Henry does not spin "Budapest"; maybe tomorrow he tells himself as he passes over the record. Henry does not believe in church, religion, or god. Organized religion is the greatest fraud ever perpetuated on humanity, Henry says to himself, his disdain of organized religion being his own consistent mumbling doxology. Henry's experiences at the Throwback Seattle Coffee Shop on one hand versus Henry's thoughts regarding organized religion on the other: are they similar? Henry sees a difference.

5.1

— I wish you wouldn't have done it, leave me that is.

— You don't understand, I didn't have a choice.

— You don't understand, there is always a choice.

— Not for me.

— Whatever! You shouldn't have done it.

— You can't understand.

— Not that I can't, it's that I don't.

— No, you don't.

— No.

—

5.2

It's my 14th birthday. I long ago stopped waiting for him to show up.

It's my 25th birthday. I think I've forgotten him. Him who? You know fucking who. Oh yeah, that who. I'd almost forgotten to remember that emptiness.

It's my 35th birthday. I bought my own damn bike. I often wonder what his life turned out to be like.

It's my 43rd birthday. Did he have other children that he did not leave? Was he ever there for someone? Are all the bad things my mother said about him true: loser, adulterer, unable to hold a job or provide for his family?

I pace. I wait. I release. I wait. I release. I leave.

5.3

Today Henry is closing on a small property close to the beach. Henry does not love his "everyday job," but it does provide him a moderate sense of security. Picking up the keys from the agent, Henry anticipates hosting his small but close group of friends for a weekend in his new home. There are pleasant moments for Henry. There have been pleasant moments for Henry. There will continue to be pleasant moments for Henry. Henry works hard to continually commingle his past and future moments into his everyday living. This is not one of Henry's best character traits.

Henry is getting sand in his wing-tipped leather shoes while unloading the contents of his car into the new beach house. Henry finds the sand both uncomfortable and awkwardly releasing at the same time. Opening a soda, Henry carefully lays a piece of paper on his kitchen countertop and begins a to-do list.

Item 1: buy beach shoes, something that won't take too long to break in.

Inside the refrigerator he places the leftover portions of his lunch. Arranging the boxes from the car into the middle of the living room, Henry realizes that he is tired. Henry grabs his jacket and heads for a walk on the beach. For now the boxes can wait.

Today Henry's grandmother passed. Henry is devastated.

Again Henry did not breed today.

Today Henry gets one day older.

6.1

—

—

—

—

—

—

—

—

—

—

6.2

I have become an old man. Today, as the end comes near, I clean out the closet. From the top shelf, I retrieve the shoebox that I have carried for too many years. I review each item. Contained within the box are the remaining pieces of my father's jacket. The leather feels worn. It felt worn before I claimed it. I hold the book in my hand, each page dog-eared and creased; the spine of the book painfully reminding me of the tattered years spent riding the bus-to-no-destination. This book—the book—*The Silver Sword* by Iran Serraillier—is a story of Joseph walking back to Warsaw after escaping a Nazi concentration camp to look for his wife and three children. Joseph's three children kept looking for their parents, never giving up hope that they would one day return. Whose story is this anyway? The writing pad contains scribbles from my father: a story or life of dreams? From my wrist, I take my father's watch and place it within the box. Today, the shoebox is dry, brittle, and weathered. Breathing in and out, each present moment in breath, a lifetime of repetitive moments in breath, I place the lid on the shoebox. I walk down the beach. I stop. Clawing at the ground, sand filling my fingernails, I find the sand both uncomfortable and awkwardly releasing at the same time. I create a hole, a whole lifetime of holes spent with a shoebox. I deposit the shoebox, cover over it, and walk away.

Singing to Bones

Michael Johnson

Her bleachwood house bleeds nailrust,
and the birds besotted with sun
nest in brambles run amuck down the pickets
gauzed in summer chaff like dusty furs.
Her `35 Ford has risen in the arms of alders
to the height of a rusty Jesus.
Hers could be a driveway to a place that never was.
Generations of game have shied
from her orchard, paid their furtive berths,
taken citizenship in the nation of shadows.
Mr. McCorkle was mauled there years ago
while she was visiting some church circle
of pie makers all acluck with gossip.
At first she shot only the bears
and left them on the stoops of the apple roots
grown to hives of bluebottle rorshach,
of nightslinks nuzzled to the bonetrough,
the feasthall cloisters of carrion ants.
From her porch she thought it brutish and fitting.
Her kills played shadowshows in the orchard alleys.
The years went, the place unboned by foxes,
and once a wolf she swore dripped moon

in the grass. Stoic, haughty, and gone.
She waited every night through the lunar quarter
and wane and ember. Everything but the wolf
returned. As all things pass, she passed.
See her watchchair, the worried heelplate
of her rifle, her doorhinges growling in the wind,
rapping at the jambs like knocks at the gate of hate
where the wind was always singing to bones,
the croon of her want, *James, James,*
where are you? And O what moon, what moon.

Charlie

Jacob Lindberg

People seldom do what they believe in. They do what is
convenient, then repent.

—Bob Dylan

"I've seen Charlie around" I
tell my mom, stiff wooden
like our pew.

"Seen him on the porcelain
face down like a street
lamp, seen him licked on
the sidewalk pick himself
up mouth first like a slack
jawed hound, seen him
smack Mary along her tan-
line shorts and lead her
home when her husband
sleeps, seen him drive the
policeman's car two bars
down and walk back, seen
him smack Loose Lacy,
snatch a warm wallet, swirl

up some drinks, spit on the
bar, spill up his guts, sweep
up his wits, and squeal
beside a brick wall."

Mom don't say much, watches
Charlie plod up to stage for his
forgiveness—a clean slate
saunter. Her mouth forming
like potholes, she don't say
much but let's me know I've
sure seen Charlie do an awful
lot, sure been close enough to
touch the sap of it all, "Get up
there and wash your hands, say
a prayer least he knows
humility is less hot than hell."

The Day I Enlisted

James Valvis

Dad told me of the time he got his draft papers.
It was during the height of the Vietnam War.
He was supposed to show at such and such place,
at such and such hour in the morning.
He was supposed to take his physical and join
the other young men serving their country.
When word got around, friends threw a party
for my father who would soon be overseas
protecting the world from the commies.
Much merriment, and the libations liberated
my alcoholic father from his short sobriety.
He drank until the morning physical
and the doctors took one look at him
and said 4F. For weeks afterward
he hung out in his basement,
not wanting the revelers to see him,
ashamed of the truth of himself,
and he might still be down there,
but eventually thirst overcame his shame.
Only fools want to be heroes anyway,
he said, and then poured himself another.

The Other Sandusky

Mike Salisbury

The mailbox is full again today. Letters packed with hate choke the opening to the point the door can't even close. Standing there at the end of his driveway, Gerry Sandusky gently tries to remove the mail without the rubber band snapping and spilling out across the road.

With his firm stance and slightly angled back, Gerry looks like a vet birthing a calf, a man playing Operation without the tongs, careful not to catch the mail on the lip of the mailbox. But the rubber band is old and lacks the intended courtesy.

Before Gerry can cradle the large mound of letters, the rubber band breaks mid-transition, sending them everywhere like confetti. The few he manages to trap in his arms are tossed to the ground in a fit of frustration.

Across the street, a kid in a basketball jersey and jean shorts watches from his BMX bike snickering, before taking a swig of Mountain Dew.

Lately, it feels like everyone is laughing at Gerry Sandusky's expense.

Gerry bends over and begins picking up each letter. Some are sent in dark blue envelopes while others are probably unintentionally white but Penn State white nonetheless. They've written his name in utter detest, a hateful font, along the lines of their own personal Hitler or Satan, or a combination of both in some cases.

The problem is he's not the right Jerry Sandusky; he's *Gerry* Sandusky, 47, a manager at JCPenney's, not a part of any football program, including their beloved Penn State.

He doesn't even watch football, college or pro, he thinks, as he goes about picking up all the hate mail.

Jerry Sandusky has thin, silver hair. His face is soft like a grandfather, a smile permanently pressed to it. If you knew him before the accusations, you might be inclined to call him "Uncle Jerry." He is disarmingly nice, gentle. Like everyone else, you would be surprised if you found out he was really a monster, a wolf in sheep's clothing.

Nothing about *Gerry* Sandusky is thin, except his hair. He rarely smiles, and no one has ever called him "Uncle Gerry."

While helping an elderly lady out at customer service recently, she belched, not directly in his face but close enough he could smell the Wendy's chili. He knew she added onions.

"Excuse me," she said, before a look of confusion struck her, a slight wobble, before vomiting all over the counter, speckling Gerry's white dress shirts in spots of dark, red blotches. The woman didn't offer to help clean up. She stood there staring at Gerry.

This Gerry Sandusky is neither wolf nor man—he's just the day manager at the JCPenney's in the Baldwin Mall and Movie Complex.

The house is quiet without Jody. Gerry dumps the mail out across the kitchen table and begins making coffee. It has been two months and the separation still hasn't set in. Working from a place of denial, he let his laundry build up to the point he ran out of clothes, and when facing the dials and options of the washer, realized this separation is very true.

This is how 16 years of marriage ends? Gerry thought, as he tried to fill the cup with detergent.

This has become his daily routine: little coffee, little hate mail. Gerry flips through the letters. It's strange to him how much people can hate someone, especially when it is someone they've never met. He doesn't blame them for hating this other Jerry Sandusky, the child molester and destroyer of college football empires. They write things like how much they hope he gets molested in prison, which is kind of twisted in Gerry's opinion. It's one thing to see a person's hate for another, but to have it addressed to you, sort of, is another.

Gerry Sandusky reads their letters, wonders what it's like to be that Jerry with an army of people actively hating him out there. It probably hurts a lot like your wife leaving, Gerry thinks and tosses the letters aside.

Karla thinks Gerry should change his name.

"That's what I'd do," she says. Karla is the night manager at JCPenney's. Part Philippian, part Canadian, she tells everyone what they should do, only politely, a regular know-it-all.

Gerry sits across from her in the break room. It smells like burnt coffee. They have tried everything to fix this, including spraying full bottles of perfume inside the microwave. The coffee proves over and over again that it's stronger than anything in the makeup department.

Gerry nods along with everything Karla is telling him. He hasn't considered changing his name. He knows Jody will, if she hasn't already. *How nice it must be*, he thinks, *to be one thing then another.* The possibilities for change are endless, and yet he can't.

"I got DirectTV installed Saturday, and the guy's name—you'll never guess—was Michael Jackson. A husky white kid named Michael Jackson—you believe that?"

Gerry did not. But he did think about that Michael Jackson compared to the real Michael Jackson, the alleged child molester and the King of Pop. He wonders if DirectTV Michael Jackson ever got mail sent to him.

Gerry Sandusky has decided to start replying to his haters, or Jerry Sandusky's haters. He starts with a form letter, politely explaining they have the wrong Gerry/Jerry, and how he's not a child molester or a football fan. He's not the man they are looking for.

In the background, the evening news relays the events of today. The mound of letters on the table is taller than Gerry. A snow covered mountain. He has to lean to the side to see around them and catch what's going on on TV.

After seven letters, he begins explaining where Jody and he went wrong, or at least where he believes they went wrong. *It's like journaling*, he thinks. This is therapy, only cheaper.

"I was wrong, okay? Maybe I should've paid as much attention to her as you do football. I should've cared more, I know that now," he writes back to David Pauley, '71 alum.

The sight of his absurdity, surrounded by these replies, Gerry wishes he were drunk. Gerry is nothing if not straight laced. He has never missed a day of work or broken one policy in the JCPenney's manager's manual. But he'd like something to blame this on other than himself. Shared blame goes a long way in these kinds of situations.

Jody is gone. This is the reality he comes back to, that he crashes into.

On the evening news, Jerry Sandusky is being lead into the courtroom in handcuffs. He's wearing an orange jumpsuit. He smiles. Even in a court of law, facing horrendous allegations, Jerry Sandusky is keeping a positive outlook.

"Why did you do this to us?" Gerry says, softly.

The news reporter looks into the camera and begins reporting the events of today's court proceedings. He finishes by telling everyone that Jerry's wife still supports him. She believes he's innocent.

The day Jody left, he could feel it in his joints, like a change in the atmosphere from an approaching thunderstorm. He helped her put her things in her Honda. Looking back on it, he wishes he hadn't. Why did he do that? He stood there in the driveway like she was leaving for a weekend at her parent's house in Lancaster. He stood there like if he waited long enough she might come back.

That's when the letters first started appearing in his mailbox. That's just after news broke what Jerry Sandusky had done.

When Gerry gets home from working the dayshift at JCPenney's, he's surprised to find the service door on the garage is busted, kicked in by an intruder. He's worried it's the Penn State fans. He dreamed the other night that they came for him like the villagers did in *Frankenstein*. He's dreaming of pitchforks and fire again.

Gerry inspects the garage. Candy wrappers and soup cans. He thinks maybe it's a raccoon or a hobo. In the corner, the boy he recognizes from the BMX bike smiles.

"Hey man, sorry about the door," he says.

Gerry is relieved it's not raccoons or football fans looking for revenge.

"I needed someplace to hide out and I thought you wouldn't probably notice."

"I wouldn't notice a kid living in my garage?"

"I've been here two weeks," he says.

Gerry's shoulders slump and he takes a long deep sigh, one that goes on long enough that the kid begins to wonder if he's deflating.

"I'm Manny," he says, popping up to shake Gerry's hand like he wants to sell him magazine subscriptions for a fundraiser for a school trip to Washington D.C.

Startled by the sudden gesture, Gerry shakes his hand, tells him his name.

"Your name is Jerry Sandusky? Like the molester?"

"No, it's Gerry with a G."

"Pretty much the same."

"I'm surprised you let him stay," Karla says, as she sprays JLo perfume in the microwave. She believes that's the issue, the microwave. Even though there's a note about microwaving your coffee, people do it anyway; Gerry does it sometimes, too.

"He's just a kid, I don't know."

"Where does he sleep?"

"In my car."

"And you never noticed?" she asks, as she sticks her head in the microwave to smell and examine.

There are a lot of things Gerry hasn't noticed lately: his weight gain, his irritability, his inability to sleep through the night without waking up multiple times worried and wondering why Jody isn't there. Things like that.

Perhaps another man, a better man, would rebuild or rebound, re-something, he thinks. He's never been that man, the kind who makes his own destiny. He wishes he could get lost in his work, like lawyers and doctors do. Work as an excuse because he's helping people. The only person he can help right now is the mom with the young boy who wants to speak to a manager about the manikins rearranged in sexual positions by the same teenagers Gerry chased off yesterday, threats of calling mall security following closely behind them.

Manny is waiting as Gerry pulls into the garage. He's wearing his basketball jersey, BMX parked in the corner. They exchange Hellos and Gerry says something about an extra McDouble. He hands the sack to Manny.

"Thanks, bro." Manny says and climbs into the backseat.

This has become their routine: Manny living out of his car, Gerry going out of his mind. He wonders if this is what it's like having kids. Jody never wanted kids. He's thankful for this now when he considers everything. Divorce can be so hard on them. Hell, it's been pretty hard on him. Why take tourists along for this spiraling vortex of doom?

Inside, Gerry opens one of the letters from the mound on the table.

"I hate your guts, you child-molesting, football-ruining scum bag."

"I do too," he replies.

"You've tarnished everything Penn State stands for," another one says.

"Everything I've got in life is tarnished. Join the club."

They all say they hate him, each and every one of them.

It's something to be universally hated, he thinks. Takes a lot of the pressure off. Lowered expectations. There's a kind of comfort in this. It's hard for him to consider a day in the future when he won't be known for someone else's crimes.

"What you need to do," Karla says, "is start dating again."

The thought of dating again makes him feel like erupting. He'd barely dated Jody, if you could actually call it "dating." More like stumbling.

Karla cleaned the break room with some of Sean "Puffy" Comb's new cologne. It has made the coffee stronger, as if through retaliation the coffee is mustering a comeback. The ghost coffee smell is angry.

"They got sites for people like you," Karla says. "My cousin got hooked up with a nice guy on the Christian Mingle. I'd start there."

"I'm not religious."

"Whacha you need to be is not picky," Karla says.

Gerry and Manny are sitting in the car, parked in the garage, sharing a tray of Oreos.

"Are you sure you don't want to go inside?"

"I prefer to kick it here," Manny says. "I'm keeping a low profile."

"Do your parents know where you are?"

"I highly doubt they even know I left, bro."

Manny twists an Oreo apart. He only eats the cream, not the cookie. There's a small pile of Oreo crumbles on the dashboard. "Where's your old lady?"

"She left."

"Yeah, I know that. But where did she go?"

"Away."

"You're better off."

"How do you know?"

"My mom's last boyfriend told her a woman's value decreases with age while a man's goes up," Manny says. "He was in real estate, I think. So, you got that going for you."

"Did your mom dump him after he said that?"

"Nope, they got married, and then he left her."

"Wow, that's messed up."

"Tell me about it."

They sit silently and eat their Oreos. *It's nice to have company,* Gerry thinks. Jody was never big on having people over, either. *Ashamed of their house,* he thinks. It's a nice ranch. Little dated. Probably could use some paint, like anything else.

They'd go over to such and such's house and stare at some over-priced piece of shit furniture, listening to Jody go on and on about Crate & Barrel this and Macy's that and about how nice everything is. He'd made the mistake once of saying, "We sell the same thing at Pennies. Probably cheaper too. Definitely cheaper."

If he'd known furniture prices would make a huge difference in his marriage, he would've opted for more expensive furniture, as if a better marriage is an option, a selection on the showcase floor.

"The worse thing that could happen to me now is Joe Paterno dies," Gerry says to Manny. "That would be great—all the kids and the death of an old man —a demigod of football—because of a man who shares my name, sort of."

"Do you know what a demigod is?" Manny asks.

"It's to be, like, just less than a god."

"Do you know that for sure or are you just making it up because you think I'll believe you because I'm a kid?"

In the break room, Karla is telling Gerry about her new relationship with DirectTV Michael Jackson.

"Do you know what the best part is?"

"Free cable?" Gerry says.

"No," Karla says, laughing. "He does the little things—flowers, opens doors, picks up the check."

Gerry has stopped listening. *We've lost our ability to consider others*, he thinks. That's what's wrong with America—consideration. And we're selfish. He thinks that, too. Inconsiderate slobs. His eyes glance over the missing persons poster on the community board. Usually it's just Craigslist items and people wanting to swap shifts. He sees the picture of Manny and stares. At first, he doesn't recognize him. Manny is wearing a tie and holding a trombone. But this is not the most surprising thing: the word "age" and next to it "14" is.

Gerry is driving home, quickly. What he needs is a plan or an explanation as to why a 14-year old boy has been living in his car. This is the problem with Gerry Sandusky: he doesn't always know something is wrong until it's too late.

In the seat next to him is the poster. He tore it off the wall and raced out of the break room while Karla was still going on about DirectTV Michael Jackson.

Maybe this is an opportunity, he thinks. Maybe this can be a win-win like their old marriage counselor used to talk about. DirectTV Michael Jackson is redeeming Michael Jacksons. Gerry Sandusky needs to redeem the other Sanduskies. He needs to show the world he's not a monster.

When Gerry gets home, Manny is inside watching TV, feet up on the sofa, shoes on.

"You're home early," Manny says.

"Yeah," Gerry says, as he picks up the cordless phone and jogs on into the bedroom. He dials Jody's number quickly. He's trying to catch his breath. He doesn't want to sound out of breath; he doesn't want to sound like old Gerry.

While the phone rings, Gerry pleads, "Please pick up, please pick up."

Jody doesn't answer.

He leaves her this voicemail: "Jody, it's me, Gerry. I know you're angry and disappointed—you have every right to be. I should've listened more. Paid more attention. We should've splurged on some better furniture," he says, then bangs the phone against his forehead. "What I'm trying to say is this: I've done something good, Jo. Something that I think will make you proud of me. And if you can see this man— The Hero—maybe you can see there's capacity in me for change," he says, feeling pretty good about that "hero" line. He digs the missing person poster out of his pocket. "I'll be at 5472 Statute Dr. at 6:00 p.m. tonight. You should be there. It's gonna be amazing, Jo. You'll see."

Gerry hangs up. His smile is huge. For once, he feels like a stud. Things are going his way. He's calling the shots.

"Hey Manny," he says. "Do you want to meet Michael Jordan?"

Jody is not there when Gerry pulls into Manny's driveway. He left a few more messages on Jody's phone and her parent's machine. Each of them patient, calm. "Please be there, Jo. Just for this. I want you to see this." She has not returned any of his calls.

Gerry looks for her anyway, scanning the crowd twice. Maybe he missed her. He will always miss her; he knows this. He wishes even now, in light of his greatest accomplishment, he could put into words exactly what it is he misses about her and in doing so make her believe in a new Gerry, a better Gerry.

A small crowd is standing in Manny's yard. There is TV lights and a reporter turning to the camera, telling the viewers about the hero returning the boy. Gerry is proud that he thought to tip off the news. Glorious, he thinks. Exactly as planned.

"You're making a big mistake, bro," Manny says.

Gerry smiles. Nods to the boy and gives him that what-do-you-know smirk. He told Manny to get into the car because he wanted to take him to meet Michael Jordan. That's right, Michael Jordan is signing autographs today at the Foot Locker in the mall, Gerry said, and because he works there, Gerry gets to cut in line and personally meet him. He's finally using sports to his advantage.

Gerry tries not to wave to the cameras like a goofball or some moron as he hops out of the car.

Play it cool, he thinks. And he does. He raises his hand and gestures to them to wait—he's got this. He considers whistling while he walks around to the other side of the car. He has found the missing boy, and even though he didn't really look for him, he's a hero. Heroes can be people who notice the obvious; they can be people like him, who do the right thing. Maybe lying to Manny was wrong, but Gerry didn't want him to get away.

As soon as Gerry opens the door, Manny bursts past him, head down. The boy has become a battering ram, his skull crashing into Gerry's gut, pushing all the air out. Gerry stumbles and sucks wind.

In a half-blur, Gerry watches Manny race up the driveway. The stuff Manny is saying is crazy talk. Words like "abducted" and "hurt" and "monster."

But he's not that Jerry.

Their faces begin to fill with horror. At first, he thinks it's just the boy, his return. It's emotional. They're just past the point of being sad and now are moving to the angry stage of grief, Gerry Sandusky is hoping.

MeSOStic (Double) You

Cindy King

thrifTshopping
halfpRicing
brownbAgging
slimfastinG
controltoppIng
JazzerCizing

tupperWaring
avOning
hoMeperming
reducEracking
haNdmedowning

couponClipping
casserOling
overtiMing
lipPursing
puRseclutching
lysOling
leMonpledging
naIlbiting
Streetcrossing
dEadbolting

nighTshifting

teetHsucking

fingErwagging

toldyousoIng

sockdaRning

goDdamning

coRnercutting

hEadshaking

bankbookbAlancing

Mother   i love

bruxism

Toni Hanner

is bruxism keeping you up / nail the door / shut hang / a curtain across the wound / feel the crowds passing through / try this / is belly fat keeping you awake / pull your navel / up and over / kiss every inch / is redshift keeping you up / gluten-free hair loss / continental / drift is the peace symbol ironic in the end / times discuss

> my body in contact with itself bruises
> dream dopplers red-splash
> sticks blown apart just before waking

Steve's Incredible Non-denominational Purgatory

Dennis Vanvick

> *"I want to put a ding in the universe."*
>
> —Steve Jobs

Steve's pissed. He's forced to mill around with the masses until they finally allow him to pass through one of two gates. Ridiculous. Ungodly rigmarole.

He's close to the front, absolutely positive he'll be ushered through the pearly gate into the flower garden, rumored to be insanely great—not the quarry entrance, rumored to be insanely horseshit. Breaking rocks is for the little people.

A gaseous, wraithlike presence forms above the throng and swoops in. The crowd parts, bowing down, sycophant style. Steve stands erect and apart—unimpressed. He's sure the wraith is simply a hologram. Clever, unless you understand the rudimentary technology.

Give Steve a savvy team of lackeys and he could easily improve the hologram, make it insanely marketable. He admits the hovering gimmick is mystifying but he'll put a team on that—harangue them, squeeze blood from turnips—and have it demystified in short order.

The wraith whispers instructions as it floats. People begin queuing up in front of each gate. What a fucked procedure! Steve will get a seat on the board and the power to fire people. Like that imbecile at the gate. Perhaps Steve may even choose to become CEO.

When the wraith reaches Steve the message is clear, "Your case remains under review. We appreciate your patience."

Awareness comes sudden, comes hard—he hasn't put a ding in the universe. The insanely great universe is pissed. And supremely unimpressed.

This Will Be for You and
You Can Call It Whatever You Like

A.R. Zarif

I myself forget what the morning is for
coming in like a comet of all quietness

it doesn't feel like anything more than
a bright stone, stillness, talking to me

with staggering breath and all I can think
is the obvious thing

how to get out of bed without going anywhere?
though I with you and you with the morning

as it settles on your face soft as powder
is hopeful

and then those small pieces of dust pulsing
in the air which are the brides of light

keep lovely memories of you
in the shape they make after you dream through them

I've never seen anything quite so pale
as the small folds of your ears

which are very pale with
the backdrop of my black hair

today I'll try for the other kind of sleeping
the kind that doesn't rely on sunlight or sugar or the sea

or mistake the sound of me walking
for any kind of applause

Not White

Jed Myers

White dogwood in bloom, faint-veined
leaf-petal quartets like fine cotton
fountained out on their stemlets

into the June sun, pointing
everywhere in the most unassuming
enticement to pollen-bearers, these

bright pennons don't have to spell it
out, I'm not white and was never
so innocent. Here, under this

dear dogwood, I'm a shade
in the range of earths, bruise-stained
and tinted hints of the breathless

blood in my veins. Never the white
skin on the warming milk before
the stir of my mother's wooden spoon.

Never like starlight, never
the white of the moon. Here under
the hung tiers of the dogwood's gown,

in the dark of my involuted gray
matter, my thought-mutters wait
for the first curled tips to tinge brown.

The Old Science and Several Lasting Threats

Luke B. Goebel

While the rest of the country was sitting on ice I was sitting on a towel with my legs spread high and out a little hand towel rolled up to make you know one those egg roll looking things.

Anyhow, my testicles were propped up on the rolled up towel a guy about to do a scrote scan on me. I could have said: my nuts my nuts my balls yadda but I don't want to give you the wrong idea that I'm some kind of real guy I'm clearly not. I feel pretty, not well not exactly feminine with him probing around me, and me pretending to not have a body, making a lot of uncomfortable male jokes about how this was not truly my livelihood in his hands but my hobby, but really feeling like my voice was sorta weak and high and my neck too thin and my clothes, well, too sloppy dressy tie and that sort of thing, me just institutionalized in the room with the drop panels and the machine and this guy teching me out scanning the eyes between my legs I have always wondered if could make children with because I'm well along this life and have never made anyone pregnant, I don't believe, and have reason to think I would have known but I've been careful—still a person wonders about babies, but who can afford them and who can condone them?

The sun had finally come back out it was 59 degrees February a fine feeling of frogs thawing out in the unfrozen earth like every spring smell you've ever known.

Kind of a Massachusettsey feel.

The guy was moving the scanner head around on one of my testicles, the right one, the right one. I had a fear of something growing. The doctor had confirmed it using the old science. Touch. There was some kind of growth or plaque or marble humming of sperm stone some bulbous thing I felt at night, felt swollen sitting with at day.

The guy with the scanner head said: I don't see anything much.

I said: I see everything! I was looking at the screen with him.

Try to remember the nature of this visit was having a man rubbing an electronic device around on my testicles through a lubricating agent with them sitting atop an egg roll towel and the machine used was the company I hate that makes nuclear products and owns media channels and makes weapons for war and suppresses the truth about wars and this guy was being so gentle with me, I was in that simple mind frame of just let's hope there is nothing wrong so we can get back to the program of figuring out then what…to do. Oh let's die already.

I said, as he drew a line from one end of the testicle to the other and another across digitally of course and took a snapshot of the screen I says I wish there was a scale to tell me weather mine were bigger or smaller than most. He just chuckled, "There's no scale," he said. "This wasn't like those metal bulls horns attached to a bulls head with the light bulbs up the wall of the game's façade that say how much passion you have," he said.

Then I started really looking at these wild images on the screen. They were like ancient Egypt, babies, two in utero sucking thumbs together, I saw wild demonic dog gods.

I said to him: God, I see all of creation.

He said: That's thinking awfully highly of yourself isn't it?

I said: No, on that screen there it's like peyote fire, it's like star matter, it's like I can see the ruins of Egypt, constellations of dog gods, visions of mayan shaman drooling priests, he said, you are a creative? I said: "do you see anything that looks dangerous? Tumorous? Tumescent, too bad, kill-me-able?" He said: "I don't see anything much."

Well we spent about a half an hour more like that, him rubbing the sensor around and around, adding more and more of the scentless lubricant.

When it was over I toweled off.

And now I'm talking into a recording device driving in the sun feeling like I've got a new license. Looking at trailer parks. Guys driving trucks with pipeliner stickers, people, thinking to myself, I ought to quit my job, start drinking again, when will I be a man about things? You know it's all we got: the sunny day the blue sky the white jet clouds, don't think too hard, this isn't that heavy of a story.

A little later on then the doctor calls me. Post script, PS, wot wot, a little extra teaser qua the doctor: before you're gone and dead for good, Dr. calls, Dr. Champion, MD Urology, seen the results, says: is this so and so such and such person who goes by the name of so forth: I say yes, it's me. He says: very interesting stuff on this reel that was sent over to me from the labo. I say yes, what did you see in there? He says: well, you're going to live a lot longer, but one thing, we are going need the Egyptian pyramids, the lake of tears, the constellations, the twins, the drooling shamanic dog heads, all of it back, along with all that other shit in there that doesn't belong to you, you know, once you're through with having them out and about.

I said, Dr., I'm going to blow up the dam I saw at Lake Powell, flood out Las Vegas, then missile the pentagon. I'm gonna hammer the central valley farm oil bastards with bombs all along the water works from the feather river to socal. I'm going to level the white house if I can manage it. All through subversive writings. I'm making serious threats against the stability of your nation. I've seen inside my nuts today, Dr., and what conclusion I've come to is this: we have been playing sane far too long. Also, I want them removed.

Trespass

John Sibley Williams

An old prison overtaken
by wild bloom and sometimes

the makeshift airfield across town
beneath the bellies of crop dusters,

though often much closer—bent
willow shaded pasture, the houses

of absent parents, wherever night
held sway—we'd grow naked

together in fugitive moments,
working the kinks out of perfection,

leaving contrails on everything
as the wind dispersed.

Nights of Me

Blaise Allen

> *When people say they miss me,*
> *I think how much I miss me too...*
> > —"Days of Me," by Stuart Dischell

When people say they love me,
I think how much more they should love me:
With publications in Ploughshares and a Pushcart,
Gallery showings, greenbacks, and metaphors of me.
Not just for my name or sparkling laughter.
Flirty-smiling-me on Facebook. All fifty-five
shades of strawberry-blonde, big-boned me.
Churlish me, humble me, smart me, the PhD.
The one that talks to dragonflies and hugs trees.
Childless Mother-Earth me. WASP twerking,
hair-flipping, mid-life Ninja, always in black
on a diet me. Crab cake making, martini shaking,
latke-noshing, breaker-of-promises-to-self-everyday
me. Dodger of church, math, and workouts.

Call me the connector, baby. Perpetual matchmaker.
Artistic arsonist: striker of flint, freer of sparks,
blower of kindle, perimenopausal, too hot to handle

combustible me. Burn the-candle-at-both-ends
3 a.m. poet, inspired insomniac me.
To musicians and people met in bars:
keeper of secrets, admissions, and names.
Non-threatening note-taker me.
The Goethals bridge of lost souls me.
My hand on a wine glass making a toast to you,
Hemingwayish me. Drink you under the table,
wooden legged stripper me. All in my head, me.
Patron Saint of throats me. Eager anticipator
of all-mighty confessions, benefactor of forgiveness
and bestowal of mercy, mercy, me.

University

Mary Miller

I sit in my office in my nice dress: cotton, black, more like a party dress than a teaching dress, but quite comfortable. Nearby, someone is moving desks. This person could move desks forever. This person can never get the desks in the right spot. They must be very large.

I consider poking around, peering into windows. I would like to scream at this person. How am I supposed to get anything done when you can't even get your fucking desks in order? But it is nearly time for me to teach and I haven't finished making notes on Ian's story and I'm hungry even though I ate an hour ago and I still don't know what to say about the story. I should have eaten more but I was with my boss and I have a hard time eating and talking at the same time. When I looked at his plate, his sandwich was gone and I couldn't believe it. I had hardly noticed him eating; it had not seemed difficult at all for him to talk and eat at the same time. But he was asking all the questions. I talked and talked. I wasn't sure he liked what I was saying. I asked him one question that came out unclear. I was sure he knew what I was asking but I hadn't asked it in the right format and he waited for me to phrase it properly but I didn't want to.

It is now eight minutes until I teach and I don't feel prepared and the woman is still moving furniture. Why do I imagine a woman? I have just imagined her. She is also in a slightly inappropriate dress. She's sweating a little. Her desks are all wrong. I will take a little bite off this Klonopin. I don't have to drink water with it, which is nice. It is just fine. I must not get any crumbs on my lips or dress, though. I'm sleepy and it's hard to know what I need. There are so many things to put in one's body. I go to the window and look out, which I have yet to do, the blinds always closed. I have a window facing a parking lot, bushes in front of it. I have my own air conditioner. I can turn it on high wear a heavy sweater. I have no idea how to use the computer and don't know if it's because I have forgotten how to use a PC or if I'm stupid or perhaps it isn't hooked up, but I have sat here before pushing buttons on a number of occasions. There is a printer, as well, but it is also useless. I have three chairs: one for me and two for other people. There have never been more than two people in my office at any time, including me. I have a bookshelf that is empty save for a wire basket that holds a single Atomic Fireball.

Reforming Dracula for a Better World

Sonnet Mondal

As a reaction against social & communal evils in India and improper forms of protest

Is the cultural diversity at stake? My mom asked.
Watching Dracula on TV I said
I wonder why he doesn't eat beef or pork
Why doesn't he prefer diversity of meat!

Her frowning eyes interrogated my unperturbed grin.

Someone has been lynched for eating beef.
My mentors are busy adding puns to their protests
returning awards and shouting on social media.
My friends with that eminent bit are waiting for their turn
to adopt the fashion in front of sardonic cameras.
My long time favourite poet too has taken up the role
Of the leader of opposition, resigning from his public service.

The market fashion of this week is to return awards, mom.
Why don't you surrender something too son? (Mom)

They have occupied the glory of awards and the glory of returning
     them too.
I wonder what to surrender!

Watching Dracula movies are a healthier choice
than graduating inside diluted walls of establishments.
I can dream of getting irrevocably intoxicated by his bite
Get bored of human blood and enjoy beef and pork for a change—
Without the fear of murderous thugs
Without caring to wonder about the glory in returning awards.

Still Life with Current Events

Ed Taylor

a big machine growls outside
a lung breathing up what is
left in the dark tunnels of water

there is heavy cutting
at the monuments

something brittle
something blurred
passing alone

a torso muffled
by satin overgarments
at the crossroad

and the graces doing
dirty work under
a bitter white star

Haunting

Morris Collins

The season you left us all in is almost over
and I woke to the doves mourning this one
final threshing. The light spreads like rot

on the damp cobble moss. Husks of honeybees
molder in the hive. There is so little
that does not diminish, and I know

that you thought when you went
that you branded yourself into permanence.

But once long ago on the road late at night
I saw a girl with one leg jumping rope
on the dock. We were friends when we were young

and I remember the year she died.
You see, darling, sometimes the dead open

our nights into their own dreams of life
and whisper to us what they fear we'll forget:
rosemarry, honeycombs, our new love's name.

Haunting

And sometimes they leave only this:
sound of a sandal striking on stone,
smell in the air of olives and hay,

summer rain coming soon.

Copper Canyon, 1968

Andrea Wyatt

We climbed the steep wall of copper canyon
in the Sierra Madre,
damp wind smelled like granite
found a cave, and bats flew out
when the dry wood caught;
cooked rice in a heavy pot, and ate
lying in our sleeping bags,
looking out the mouth of the cave, down, into the darkness
while sheets of rain pounded the twisted yucca and cactus.
there were peace talks in Hanoi,
we hadn't heard news for a long time,
and we talked about what it would be like
when the war was over.

Creeper

J.M. Jones

Creeper is back again. He's in the studio behind her. Alex can feel his presence even before he opens his mouth to speak. His presence is singular, unique, different from the men in the carpenters union that rent space in the building. He brings a coldness to the room, discomfort, and has since the first time he stepped through her door and she'd started to think of him as Creeper. The others don't know she calls him that, but they know he's Creeper nonetheless. She's mentioned his behavior, and none of them likes a guy who acts that way.

Creeper sidles in and taps on her fish tank. *Tap, tap, tap. Tap, tap, tap.* She wants to yell, "Stop it!" But fears offending him. As of now, she's managed to evade intimacy, turn down his invitations, and she's always had excuses to save his pride. They exchange pleasantries when passing in the hall. She answers his questions without asking any of her own. But she worries what would happen if she ever has to reject him outright.

Two groups of three: *tap, tap, tap*; *tap, tap, tap.* What's that? Obsessive compulsive? If so, it's not his fault, and she lets him tap but keeps herself angled away until he speaks.

"Your fish had babies," he says.

She puts on a flannel shirt to cover the tank top she's wearing.

"Yeah, I saw that."

Alex brought the fish tank to add some life to the room, which consists of bare concrete floors and two thick supporting pillars on which she's tacked a calendar and flyers for a gig her husband's band is playing next week. She's hung a clock too, but otherwise, the cold metal ducts crisscross above her head, a mesh of wires and tubing running back and forth. It is a workshop after all, an old factory down in Kensington. And though she'd worried in adding the fish tank that her landlord would tell her they don't allow pets, he hadn't said a thing. No one had, until now. Does Creeper think she hadn't noticed? That the fish had babies right when he walked in the room? He's making small talk. But even his most innocuous comments test her patience.

"You should keep them separate when they're born," he says. "Or the mama eats the babies." And there it is. What she's expecting. Creeper crossing a line. She glances his way, and he's smiling, standing with that unsettling gaze, as if he's just made the most perplexing remark in the world.

The problem with Creeper is all feeling. He's done nothing that warrants action. Plenty of guys have that vibe about them, an awkward gait, a strange way of delivering sentiments that implies neither irony nor sincerity, leaving the listener uncertain how to respond. She doesn't like the way he looks at her, the way he feels in her space. He's unpleasant, yet booting him out makes her feel bad, especially since she welcomes everyone else. Creeper has this patchy beard that runs along his jaw into a faint goatee that hides his lips. When he smiles, it's not a smile but a grimace. He looks pained, unattractive. Yet, last time she checked, being unattractive wasn't a crime. He also has strange gray eyes, beady with bags beneath. They're too large and seem likely to tumble out any moment. Whenever he visits, he scans the room and blinks a lot. He blinks too much, and this makes her wonder if he's got some kind of condition. Maybe Asperger's. And what's she supposed to do, ban the guy with Asperger's? Still, it bothers her enough that she mentions it to her upstairs neighbor Bill.

"Want me to beat his ass?" Bill says, jokingly.

"No," she replies, "I think he's got a condition. Some sort of social problem."

Reichenbach Restorations. This is what she calls her company. *Reichenbach.* She likes the sound of the word. It evokes classicism, confidence, nostalgia. It evokes the old world and antiques. *Reichenbach.* She's built this business herself. And she's proud of that, finding a niche in a world with a skillset traditionally afforded men. She found the space and assembled a client list, and she's delivered. She's restored furniture—chairs, tables, wardrobes. She's good at what she does, capable, and she can handle this, too. She can handle Creeper. He's just a guy, a blip, a bump in the road. She's here to work, and he can't make her leave. She keeps telling herself she's not going to move just for him.

The next day Creeper shows up with fish. In both hands, he hoists a plastic bag with one fish floating inside each. He doesn't explain why he thinks she needs more fish when hers have had babies. He simply offers her the bags and she accepts. "Thanks," she says. He doesn't smile, just nods. He goes out and down the hall to his room, and she watches him go. She has lots to do, so she opens the tank and places the bags in the water. It feels strange accepting a gift from someone she doesn't like. But she can't refuse. They're only fish. And once the water temp inside the bags matches the tank, she'll tear them open and let the fish swim out. She's no expert, but the ones he brought her look nice—sleek black bodies with elegant fins, a bluish hue on their bellies. They swim around in the bags, back and forth, back and forth, and Alex returns to what she'd been doing before.

When she leaves that night, she hears the door to Creeper's studio creak. At least, she thinks she hears it. She imagines him peering out. The hall is dingy, lit by fluorescents. She locks up and looks at his door and strains to see if it's open. A closed door in the building generally means the occupant isn't there. The carpenters, when they're in, keep the doors open, and this fosters an air of affability. They stop by each other's spaces to chat. But Creeper never opens his, even when it's summer and they need the doors open to create a cross draft.

Alex considers knocking, saying thanks for the fish, but worries that this might be invading his space. Although he visits her workshop frequently, he's never invited her to his. He's invited her for coffee and dinner, but never to visit. Maybe he's living there, sleeping in his studio, which she knows is a lease violation. She thinks she sees a lighted space at the edge of his door, someone peeking out. Before leaving, she raises a hand. "Good night," she says. But the words echo back and the sound of her voice frightens her.

"Maybe you should get a Taser," her husband suggests.

They've met up at El Bar, and they're outside at one of the picnic tables. Alex's best friend Amanda sits beside her shaking her head.

"They're illegal," she says.

She hasn't seen much of Amanda recently. She's been so focused on building her business she hasn't had time to socialize. They talk on the phone and instant messenger, which means Amanda's up to speed on Creeper. But it's good to get out for an evening, socialize.

"That doesn't mean you can't get one," her husband says, "My sister has one. I can ask where she picked it up."

"I'm not sure I'd want one," Alex says. "I'd end up Tasing myself."

Steven isn't tough. If Creeper attacked her, she doesn't think her husband could help, even if he *was* there. But there's something in this type of situation that elicits the same reaction from men—defensiveness, violence.

"It's a screwed up situation," Amanda says. "But he sounds like a punk. I bet you could take him."

Alex laughs. She's stronger than she looks. She used to beat guys at arm wrestling. She discovered the talent back in her barhopping days. She'd challenge them. They'd look at her thin arms and think she was joking. They'd give a cocky smile and take the whole thing lightly and then start to lose. They'd exert some force, but by then, it was too late. She'd have their hands hovering near the table, and it's hard to come back from that. Come to think of it, this was another thing that worried her about Creeper. She wasn't sure how seriously to take him. What if he had her down before she realized, if he surprised her the way she'd surprised these guys? Still, Steven's suggestion seemed extreme. A Taser? What if she inadvertently hit him with four hundred volts? Those things gave people heart attacks. If she read the situation wrong, she could kill him.

When Alex arrives at her studio the next morning, she's hung over and her fish are dead.

As they'd moved on to other subjects the previous evening, she found herself ordering beer after beer. This was partially due to seeing Amanda for the first time in ages, but she'd also hoped to bury the anxiety all that talk of Creeper had caused. When it was just, "He needs his ass kicked," she wasn't as worried as when her husband had brought up Tasers. It seemed to enhance Creeper's menace, to make the threat of his presence palpable. A weird guy might need to be threatened to make him back off. But Tasers were needed to put down a rapist. And she'd never coupled Creeper with that until now. To her mind, rapists were masked men lurking in parks at night, though she knew this flew in the face of statistics. Most victims were raped by someone they knew. She'd even been acquainted with a few girls, tangentially, who'd been raped in college. Or, she'd heard they'd been raped. It was rumored. They hadn't told her themselves. It was more, "Do you know what happened to so-and-so…" She'd never heard of charges levied or arrests. It seemed that so-and-so kept it to herself, told her friends, but not the authorities, and Alex had sworn when she heard this that she'd never let it happen to her.

But wrong place, wrong time, and who knew?

Still, she could prevent it now. She insisted on this. She drank more and more and talked of her time arm wrestling, and as she bragged, this one guy had challenged her.

"Let's see what you got," he said.

They locked hands over the table.

"You ready?" she said. "On three."

As she strained, she couldn't stop thinking, *If I beat him, I'll be safe. If I beat him, I'll be safe.* She had him, too. Not quite pinned, but close to the table. The problem was that this guy took her seriously and hadn't fooled about. She had leverage and swung his fist to the side. But he was stronger and put up enough resistance to push it back. He was trembling. Their arms shook. She saw it coming, but still, it surprised her when it happened. Her hand hit the table.

"You're good," he said. "You have this thing where your wrist locks. You sort of bend it like this."

"Is that illegal?"

"No, it's a decent technique. Smart."

his made her smile. She was smart. She could get by using her head, though she didn't know what it meant that she'd lost. Did it mean her concerns over Creeper were founded? She'd had another and another and got drunk and now this: dead fish.

Had Creeper known it would happen? Had he bought these fish as retribution for turning down his invitations for coffee? No, that was crazy. She's married, and he knows that.

She looks into the water. Bubbles come up off the filter. The sleek black bodies of the fish Creeper gave her float on the surface and the baby fish are gone. Then she sees the others, the parents of those babies, her original fish. They're swimming at the bottom of the tank, moving among the rocks and plastic plants embedded in gravel. Had *they* killed the black fish? There wasn't any way to tell. Still, it seemed better than the possibility Creeper had knowingly brought her a breed that ate babies and killed themselves.

She's almost in tears but holds back. Right then Bill walks in. She forgot she'd left the door open. But then, she always leaves it open. Maybe she should close it, lock herself in when she's here. She'd be safer.

"Hey," he says, "What happened to your fish?"

He takes a closer look and says, "I see."

"What?" she says. "What do you see?"

"They're Japanese fighting fish. Haven't you seen *From Russia with Love*?"

"What?"

"*From Russia With Love*. James Bond. In close quarters, they fight to the death. Didn't you know?"

"Do you think I'd put them in there if I knew?"

Bill steps back and holds up his hands.

"Sorry."

Alex runs a hand through her hair.

"No, it's been a rough night. I got together with a friend I haven't seen in a while, and we were out late. I had a bit too much to drink, and now this."

She gestures at the tank.

"No, I get it. It's messed up. I just thought they might have told you at the store."

Did they tell Creeper? If they did, he must have known, but why wouldn't he mention it? Was it a prank? Did they assume that since he was buying the fish, he'd done his research? Maybe the salesman didn't know either. It's not like everyone watches James Bond.

"They might have," she says. "But I didn't buy them. It was Creep…"

Right then, she feels guilty. She hadn't meant to use this name. It just sort of fell from her lips. But Bill catches on.

"He did this?" He stares at the tank in disbelief. "Shit! You want me to talk to him?"

He means it, but she's worried. Does he mean talk or intimidate? Bill's a big guy. Setting him off on Creeper could prove just as bad as using a Taser. And if Creeper's been bullied his whole life, it might make things worse. She doesn't want this to get any worse. She wants damage control, a friendly way to turn his attentions elsewhere. She knows that something's wrong with him, but she's not sure what.

"No," she says. "I can handle it. I doubt he knew. He doesn't seem the James Bond type."

But she doesn't talk to him. Over the next few days, she doesn't see him. She hasn't started to lock her door, but she leaves it open only a crack, so people have to knock, and Creeper doesn't. She doesn't pursue him either. A couple of times, she hears footsteps in the hall, but they pass by. Maybe it's not even him. Maybe he's moved. Maybe he's cleared out. But that's wishful thinking. She trusts her instincts, and somehow she's certain he hasn't left.

One night as she's leaving, she thinks she sees him. The El train runs right above the studio, and when she walks to her car, she goes beneath the pillars and shadows of the rail line. Every once in a while, a train runs past and makes a deafening clatter, but right then, it's quiet. A car passes, then another. It's six-thirty, but the street's not heavily trafficked, and that's all she sees—two cars, and then she's alone. The sound of her footfalls echo. She feels someone's following her. Is it him? She stops and turns, and the sound stops. She sees her shadow move and jumps. It's not that late, but it's dark. If it happens now, she can run. She has sneakers on and avoids the blind spots—alleys and doorways, the spaces between the cars. The street is composed of businesses, and the businesses are closed, so there's no one around. She needs a jump, a head start. If he comes at her, she needs to see him first. She can fight if she has to, but it's best to run. She hears footsteps, and this time they're not hers. She looks for the source, but doesn't see one. She hears a car door slam and an engine start, and not far off, a car pulls out. It passes, and in the glint of the streetlight, she sees a man sitting inside, but can't tell from the glare who it is. It could be him. But she can't say for sure.

As a teen, she'd been bullied in school. She can't remember the names of the girls, just the feeling they gave her when she passed them in the hall, the way she'd wanted to shrink from sight, how she'd longed to become invisible. Dealing with Creeper feels like that. She hears footsteps in the corridor, and whether they're his or not, she wants to dissolve. She doesn't know what he's planning to do, but she refuses to become a victim. She takes inventory of the items in her shop, tools she could use as weapons—hammers and hacksaws, screwdrivers, box cutters, a nail gun, a drill. She knows that anything she can use against him, he can use against her, so she keeps them concealed in drawers close at hand. She wears her tool belt everywhere, and sometimes, when she's alone, she practices swinging her hammer. She's had enough of the fear and paranoia. She hopes he'll leave her alone. That's all she wants. She hates that it has to be cruel, but it can't be helped.

In the meantime, Alex throws herself into refurbishing an old woman's dollhouse. It's a passion project for her. It helps her forget that Creeper is down the hall. Most of her jobs involve restoring furniture, reupholstering chairs, refinishing tables and desks. And while that requires skill and finesse, the intricate work she's doing on the dollhouse takes a deeper focus. The world falls away as she replaces the green and white striped wallpaper above the wainscoting in the kitchen. She forgets herself as she fashions lace curtains for the windows. She sands down the dining room chairs and table and stains the wood and adds polish.

She wasn't planning to take the project at first, since it falls outside the spectrum of what she usually does. But the woman had been referred by another customer, and Alex tries to do all she can to keep her clients happy. Then too, the woman approached her with such hope. This was her dollhouse from youth. It had been stored in an attic and subject to wear, and she had asked Alex to restore it so she could hand it down to a granddaughter. What could Alex say? She took it on, and it's only now, as she's putting the finishing touches on, a week since she last saw Creeper, that she notices the smell. She wonders at first if a rat crawled behind the wall and died. But as she moves about, searching for its source, she follows the scent to the door. The smell grows more pungent toward the hall. She follows it to Creeper's studio and considers knocking, but doesn't.

It's only a bit after five o'clock, so Bill should be around. He's usually here until six, just a flight of stairs above, so she turns and goes. She isn't sure what's behind the door, but she doesn't want to face it alone. She's forgotten all her plans, the tool belt, those weapons that aren't weapons. She's scared and knows that anyone would be. Does he have a body stuffed in there? Has he killed someone? Or *is* it him? God, she'd feel bad if it was. All her suspicions, then this. She climbs the concrete stairs. Her footfalls echo.

"Bill!" she calls out.

He'll know what to do, though she has to admit, she hates this, hates that she can't handle it herself. After all, she knows how to pick up a phone and call the cops. She just doesn't want to. She's done this before, gone to see Bill. But it's usually him that comes to her. What's the difference, she wonders, between Bill and Creeper? She's never considered this before. They both come and stand at her door and talk, but the one's okay and the other is...

Dead? Could he be dead?

Sad to say, she feels some relief at this, and it's horrid. Horrid to hope someone's dead just so they'll leave you alone. And yet, she hates him. She can't deny it. She hates him. Hates him for killing her fish. Hates him for making her feel small and scared. Does this make her a terrible person? She judged him and wrote him off and can't even say she's sorry about it. She hurries and reaches the top of the stairs and knocks at Bill's door, though it's wide open.

"Bill," she says, "It's Creeper. There's a smell. It's coming from his room."

Bill doesn't hesitate but comes right away, and as they rush along, she thinks, *he's got someone stashed in there. There's someone beneath the floorboards.* This is ridiculous though. They don't even have floorboards. Just a thick slab of concrete. Yet, something is rotting in there. Once they reach the first floor, there's no doubting it. Bill turns and nods. "Go call the cops," he says. But there's no way she's leaving now. She's going to see it through. She's going to stay at Bill's side.

He knocks, and when Creeper doesn't respond, he jiggles the knob. "Hey! Hey! Is anyone in there!"

He waves Alex to the side.

"I'm going to break it down."

"Are you sure you should do that?"

Still, she steps away. She wants to see.

Bill backs up and lowers his shoulder. With all his weight, he slams into the door and it gives way. They stand, framed by the door, silent, staring. It's dark, but the hallway light seeps in, and they see a figure, dangling, quiet. Alex hears a few flies buzzing about, but she can't see them. And once the smell hits full on, both she and Bill take a step back. She'll never know what he meant by the fish, whether or not he'd intended to scare her, if they served as a warning sign or some kind of sick goodbye. But her instincts had been right. There'd been something wrong. She and Bill stand, staring in. Alex puts a hand to her mouth, and holds it there, cupping the animal sounds of shock and fury that are coming out. *Creeper,* she thinks, *Creeper, what have you done?*

A Taxidermist's Son

Randolph Parker

You sat at your workbench backing the hide
of a fox in good fur with arsenic paste
to protect it, you'd say, against the ravages of living things.

I heaved words your way, but they fell
short, like everything else.
The animals, fearless now, watched you—witnessed

your passion for fur and formaldehyde.
They knew your touch, your smoothing of feathers.
An endless possibility of glass eyes glowed in the bins.

Finally, you motioned me to the bench.
I laid my dog down, blood already
clotted on her head, guilt welling up.

I surveyed all the animals sympathetically
nodding in the shadows, their perpetual flights,
steady stalking, arched backs, alert eyes,

Infinite instinct with white teeth
ready to grab hold of here and now
and hold on forever.

But all you could say was, "Dogs are for burying."
And we went back behind the shack, put Blackie
into a bag and began to dig in the clay and kudzu.

With white lines on your fingernails, face
deathly pale in the surprised sun, you
were dizzied by the shovel's weight

and I by the feeling that I was bound to you
only by that smothering endless vine
of unintended consequences.

louisiana

Toni Hanner

Small preparations / plugging in / sweeping the eyes / suffocating culture's velvet / rodeo buckles / wet car windows / we wear glass / i can see / you all i want to / i was afraid i would be called upon to be / embarrassed i / stripped down to a lie

there is a room full of hysterics another
with women who cut themselves
starlings cuss and mutter in the trees

A Handsome Woman

Mary Miller

Three weeks after I moved to this town, my boyfriend broke up with me over the phone. He let me do it. He let me believe I had some say in the matter. He said he was going to take half a Viagra and masturbate. That's all he had left. I said that was the saddest thing I'd ever heard, and it really was one of the saddest, or most pathetic. He said I was a handsome woman—not pretty, not beautiful—but handsome. Maybe he said very handsome. He was saying that I was sure to find someone. He, however, would not find someone so easily, not on the farm or in the fields or in the farm stores where he went to buy and sell feed and equipment and talk about farm stuff. His sister is sorry and every so often she sends me pictures she took of the property on which I live, mostly pictures of trees and geese and clouds, but also of odd things, like a turtle skull she found by the pond, one of its eye sockets weirdly larger than the other. I wonder why she keeps sending me pictures of things I can look out my window and see. Here are the things that are yours, she seems to be saying. See how beautiful? She is a psychiatrist. I look at her pictures, study them, and then go outside and try to place them.

The Real Story

Joan Wilking

He picked her up on the Maryland Turnpike, a girl who, at first glance, looked to be in her teens, but, when she got in, the lines that spider webbed from the corners of her eyes gave her away, thirties, early forties even. Her jacket was the same shade of orange as the late fall trees by the roadside. It was wool, pilled and open at the shoulder seam on one side. Otherwise, her hair was clean and her nails shaped and polished pale pink. Funny, he thought later, that he noticed those things. Were men supposed to notice those kinds of things? When she smiled at him her teeth were white and straight.

"Evie," she said, pronouncing the first three letters with a long "e" which made him laugh.

"I hope you didn't bring an apple. I'm Adam. I'm only going as far as Charlotte."

"Perfect," she said and pulled a half full bottle of a purple sports drink out of her bag.

She twisted the top off and held it out.

"Sip?" she said.

"No thanks."

He didn't mean to be rude but she was a stranger and for all he knew whatever was in the bottle could be laced with drugs, something he'd sworn to avoid, or was sitting so long it had fermented into a toxic brew. She guzzled the drink, wiped her mouth with the back of her hand and sighed.

She held the bottle out to him again and said, "You sure?"

"I am," he said.

And he was, especially after watching her linger with the bottle to her lips. Who knew where that mouth last had been? They drove into the glare of the sun. He pulled the visor down, fished around for his sunglasses and put them on. She turned her head to look out the window without having to squint.

"Isn't this time of year sublime," she said. "Look at that sky. And those trees."

She retrieved a pouch from her bag, unzipped it and pulled out a tube of lipstick and a small mirror. He side glanced her applying it first to her upper lip, then the lower, until her mouth was a startling slash of red. He thought she was prettier au naturel. There was something cheap about the color that accentuated the shabbiness of her torn coat.

The exit came up so fast he almost missed it. It had been a long time since he'd driven to Charlotte. He used to be more familiar with the roads. At the end of the ramp he said, "Where to?"

"Here's fine," she said.

"But there's nothing here. You sure?"

He'd slowed down. There were a couple of cars behind him, so he turned off the ramp and pull over onto the shoulder.

"Give me a minute," she said. "I've got to make a call."

She got out of the car and stood leaning against the door, phone to her ear. As she spoke, her jacket fell open and he could see that she was wearing a sparkly black dress with a plunging neckline. Her cleavage was impressive, too impressive for such a small woman. Probably fakes, he thought as he fought the sensation in his pants. He couldn't hear what she was saying at first. But as her voice rose he caught bits and pieces.

"I told you one fifty was my bottom line if I had to travel. Taxi? You crazy? I had to hitchhike here."

She babbled on a while more before she got back in.

"Thanks," she said. "My pimp is on his way to pick me up."

Just like that she said it, as if she could have been telling him she'd hitchhiked to Charlotte to visit her mom.

"Damned internet. Everyone wants something for nothing," she said. "Back in the day you could stand on a corner and negotiate. Now it's all online."

"No way I'm just leaving you here," he said.

"Why the hell not? I can take care of myself."

She reached into her purse and pulled out a can of pepper spray. She held it up and waved the can around, he could feel himself flinch.

"And I carry more serious fire power if it ever comes to that," she said and dropped the can back into her bag. It made metal on metal clink when it hit bottom. He was afraid to ask her to elaborate. Her phone buzzed and lit up to reveal a text.

"Oh, great," she said. "He's running late."

She glanced up and down the barren roadway. Cars and tractor-trailers with giant wheels sped by. The shoulder was bare earth with a bit of gravel. It sloped down sharply. There was no place to stand.

"How late?" Adam asked.

"An hour. An hour and a half."

She started to open the door.

"Look," he said. "There's got to be a gas station or a convenience store somewhere nearby."

She pulled the door closed. "I wouldn't mind a cup or coffee and maybe a little something to eat." She gave him a wink. "Got to keep your strength up in my line of work."

He checked his mirrors for cars coming off the exit ramp and down the highway before pulling out. About a mile on there was a Circle K. She picked a salad out of one of the cases and got coffee. He grabbed a tuna salad sandwich, some salt and vinegar chips and a Coke. The clerk rang them up together and Adam started to pay.

"What are you doing?" Evie said. "It's not like this is a date." She rummaged around in her bag for her wallet and handed him enough cash to cover hers. The bag was a big cloth sack. He'd already seen the sports drink and the pepper spray. He wondered what else she had in there in addition to the extra fire power. A change of underwear? Condoms? Antiseptic wipes?

There was no place to sit so they went back to the car. She pried the clear plastic top off of the salad and balanced it on the console between the front seats.

"Yuck," she said, picking through the vegetables. "Scallions. I hate scallions. And will you look at this lettuce." She held up a piece that was brown on the edges and wilted. By the time she was through, all that was left was a handful of lettuce leaves, a couple rounds of carrot, two tomato wedges and some cucumber. They ate and drank in silence.

She dumped the rejected salad components into the empty bowl and snapped the top back on. He took all the trash and dumped into the can in front of the store.

When he got back in, she said, "So where are you headed?"

"To my parents. It's been awhile."

"Why's that? You not get along with your folks?"

He had to think before he answered. What kind of story was there to tell? He could say there was no good reason why he'd been away so long. That he was simply headed home for a visit. Other people did that. They went home just because there were friends and family there, people they loved. Or he could make something up, a depressing family emergency. Or he could tell her some semi-accurate version of the last couple of years. How he'd been floundering around since he got out of college. That there had been a girlfriend, but it didn't work out, and a couple of dead end jobs. But he was still hopeful. That last part was stretching the truth.

"Nothing like that," he told her. "I was working. Up north. And then in Atlanta."

Her phone lit up with a text again and she tapped out a reply.

"He's almost here. You've been so nice, if you want me to give you a quickie…"

It took a second for him to get the gist of what she was offering. It was daylight. The sun was high in the sky. The brightness exaggerated the color of her mouth. Her lipstick was half bitten off after eating, and he could see she was wearing makeup that stopped at her jawline, where her neck turned stringy and pale.

"I think I'll hold out for something more wholesome," he said, and wanted to choke back the words as he said them. At least he hadn't said: "…*someone*…" He searched for something else to say.

"What I meant was…I appreciate that. I really do. Maybe some other time."

He intended it as an apology, instead it came out as a lame croak. Not nearly good enough to make up for the way he'd insulted her. She leaned towards him and for a minute, from the look on her face, he was afraid she was going to slap him, or worse. He kept an eye of her hands and her bag, which was on her lap.

"Well listen to you, Mr. Clean Cut."

She sucked the last swallow of coffee out of her cup.

"So tell me. Where have you been?"

"Uh, here and there," he said.

When she reached into her bag he reached for the door handle and was prepared to jump out of the car. She pulled out a small white cube. He slumped in relief.

"You see this. Where do you think it came from?"

She handed it to him. At first he thought it was a drug laced sugar cube, but it was smooth and cool.

"Pompeii. In Italy," she said. "You ever been to Pompeii? I have. There was a bunch of workmen raking those up. Do you know what it is?"

He stared at the thing and said, "No." It felt like some kind of stone.

"That's marble from one of the mosaics that used to be there. They moved them all to a museum in Naples, but some pieces were buried so deep when Vesuvious erupted and were left behind. One of the workmen told me that even after hundreds of years, they still keep working their way up to the surface. He gave me a handful. No charge."

Adam held the marble cube up. It looked like one half of a pair of dice without the black dots.

"How about Paris? You ever been there? Or Cancun? Or Rio? And I bet you've never been to India, to the Ganges. What a zoo that place is."

She sounded angry.

"Actually I haven't been much of anywhere," he said, which was true.

Her coat was hanging open and the curve of her breasts made him wish he'd accepted her offer. If had he would have avoided their conversation. She crumpled her empty coffee cup and shoved it into a pocket in the door.

"Well I have," she said. "Next trip is already booked. I'm taking the kids to Disney, the one in France. Is that wholesome enough for you?"

"You've got kids?"

Oh, God, he thought, and said, "So sorry, that came out wrong, too."

The air in the car smelled of salad dressing and tuna fish. He was starting to understand what claustrophobia felt like. He waited for her to chastise him, to tell him that in her spare time she was a preschool teacher, had a house in suburbia, something as unexpected as her story about trekking around Pompeii, but before she could say anything, a silver Volvo station wagon pulled up next to her side of the car.

"Here he is," she said flatly.

The guy behind the wheel put the window down and called over to her.

"Sorry I'm late."

He waved to Adam and Adam gamely waved back. Evie gathered up her things. The guy and the car were not what Adam expected. He was white, wearing an Atlanta Braves baseball cap, not the broad brimmed velvet hat with a plume Adam had imagined. And he was young. He could have been some college kid if Adam didn't know better. Or who knew? Maybe he *was* a college kid, working his way through. Evie got out without even saying goodbye. She climbed in with the pimp who leaned over and gave her a chaste kiss on the cheek before he backed out of the parking space and drove away.

Adam was left holding the little cube of marble. It wasn't more that a half-inch square on each side. He pictured the volcano, Vesuvious, erupting, the lava, hot and glowing, flowing into the city, all those poor people running for their lives.

As he drove across the parking lot and waited for the traffic to open up, he remembered something he studied in high school, something else about Pompeii. How there was a neighborhood full of brothels. The women who worked them were slaves, locked in to keep them from running away. It didn't seem like that for Evie, she seemed to have free rein. But who was he to know anything about her outside of the couple of hours they'd spent together in his car. Still, once he was on the road, he couldn't get the image out of his head; a woman sprinting to escape the lava, her dress on fire, her hair spiking flames the same shade of orange as Evie's ragged coat.

He cursed his naiveté. She'd been hitchhiking. Her clothes were torn. Some of the sequins on her dress were hang off. Who was she kidding? Pompeii? Euro Disney? He brightened up a bit as he turned off the highway onto the tree lined street that lead to the turn up to the plain white house where he'd spent such an unremarkable childhood. He pulled into the driveway, still holding the piece of mosaic. He rolled it around in his fingertips a couple of times before he opened the lid of the console and surveyed the mess of candy wrappers, soiled napkins and gas station receipts. He changed his mind and didn't drop it in. Instead, he held it up and inspected it. He'd been so sure when Evie first handed it to him that it was a sugar cube soaked in LSD or ecstasy and for an instant he actually considered getting stoned with her.

What he'd told Evie about himself was true only in so far as he went. He *had* worked up north and in Atlanta, but the last year he'd lived in a haze of drugs and self-doubt so intense some days he couldn't even will himself to get dressed. Finally, Caroline, the girlfriend, who he was sure deserved better than him, had kicked him out of the studio apartment she paid for with money from her job bagging groceries at the supermarket where he met her. He was home, if he still had the right to call it that, because there was nowhere else left to go.

Now he was at the head of the walk, holding what he saw as the perfect prop. With a bit of revision—a few added details to make him look better—he'd have an amusing story to tell his parents to deflect their inevitable questioning. *"So son, now that you've bombed out of yet another job and fucked up your relationship with a perfectly good girlfriend, what do you plan to do with your life?"* Of course, they'd never have the nerve to be so blunt. And he didn't need them to tell him what was obvious, the window for making something of himself was closing down. Given how the day had gone so far, the irony wasn't lost on him. It was embarrassing that a forty something hooker, he picked up by the roadside, had her shit more together than he did. He dropped the bit of stone into the pocket of his jeans. With each step closer to the house he could feel it digging into his thigh.

He wouldn't tell them about Evie. Not the real Evie. He'd make her into a waif, who needed his help to get back to her family in Charlotte after meeting some guy on the internet and following him to Italy. But his mother was sure to turn a story like that into a lecture about why he should never pick up a hitchhiker. He could say that she was a friend of a friend to whom he'd given a ride. That it turned out she was a really interesting person, beautiful, well educated, a world traveller (thus the relic from Pompeii), someone he might like to see again. But that would lead to them bugging him about when he was going to call her, since he knew they were always hoping that some nice girl would come along to straighten him out.

It was the real story that made his mouth go dry and his stomach twist, the realization that no made up story, no tall tale, no matter how convincingly he told it, could delay the inevitable telling of the truth. He stood on his parents' stoop, his heart thudding in his chest. The leaves on the bushes flanking the front door were shaped like tongues of flame and were colored to match. He pulled the stone cube out of his pocket, knelt down and pressed it into the dirt next to one of the brilliant shrubs before he took one last deep breath of the crisp fall air, stood up, rang the bell and waited for them to welcome him in.

Just time I figure

Donald Levering

to cross the early morning street
and go into the store
to change a bill for bus fare

I rush across against the light
as a yellow car approaches
and sparrows in the swirl

of mating flight
chance into its path
and one is hit

The car speeds on
and in my hurry I don't spare
the time to move the bird

Just a moment inside
making change
I return to the street

where already a crow
picks at the struck sparrow
before the bus arrives

erasing me from the scene

Walking on My Birthday

James Valvis

Some years back I might have taken time off
and skipped my walk, which is a challenge
due to my plantar fasciitis, but not this year,
not after having had to miss, with busted heels,

two months of walking as I hobbled around.
Rest is a young person's passion, but work is loved
by those nearer the end, to do the old thing well,
or even to do it at all. Because I chose to walk,

I saw at Timberlake Park such a sunrise,
purple sky streaked with red and water
so brackish blue it broke my heart so that
I made an exception and stopped my walk

to sit on a stump to watch, until it changed,
grew lighter. After that, I made my way home,
promising to tell the world about it, to do
this other thing I can still do, this joyful work.

"Samira Halawi"

Jennifer Zeynab Maccani

The girl was wearing red when she jumped from the overpass. Mrs. Cassandra LeBlanc never remembers color but *that*, she remembers. The girl looked like a streaky star on her way down. Her legs splayed out, stretched behind her. She looked like a rocket. She looked like she was on fire.

Mrs. LeBlanc slowed the car to watch the girl fall. It all happened so fast, and Mrs. LeBlanc had never seen anything like that before, had never been so close to death. It was mesmerizing. She lost sight of the black-haired girl when she got close because of the roof of the car.

That was when Mrs. LeBlanc thought, *She's going to hit me.*

It happened fast. The girl rolled rag-doll across the windshield. There was black hair everywhere. Three days later, Mrs. LeBlanc pulled clumps of black hair out from the grate, from under the rubber of the windshield wipers, from where the windows met the frame. Yesterday, her husband found a scrap of red polyester wedged into the air intake. It was pleated, thin as gossamer.

A week after the jump—another Thursday—a reporter from the Tribune knocks on Mrs. LeBlanc's door. He wants her story for the front page. Mrs. LeBlanc asks them how all this happened in the first place. She asks them why the little black-haired girl jumped from the overpass. The reporter tells Mrs. LeBlanc that he doesn't know why. He tells Mrs. LeBlanc that the girl's father didn't even know it happened until someone called the prison to tell him. The girl didn't leave a note. She just unlocked her mother's car door, tumbled out, and jumped.

The *Tribune* runs Mrs. LeBlanc's story on the front page the next day, just as they'd promised. Katerina Turner sees the headline when her father discards half the newspaper, looking for the sports pages: *Samira Halawi, age 15, leaps to her death from interstate overpass.*

Katerina picks up the newspaper from the trash and murmurs, "She wasn't fifteen. She turned sixteen on Thursday."

She's seen Samira's name before, heard it repeated by her teachers and over the loudspeaker with varying mispronunciations. Samira never corrected them. Only Katerina repeated the name under her breath, wondering why she didn't have the courage to stand up and correct them, wondering why neither she nor anyone else in their class ever wanted to sit at Samira's lunch table.

Yesterday, Principal LeBlanc came on the loudspeaker and announced Samira's death. She said the school would have someone to talk to kids who were upset, kids who didn't understand.

But no one seems to be upset. That's what troubles Katerina most: the way everyone goes on with their lives like nothing has happened. Like no one is missing. Like little Ashley Forster sat at Samira's desk all along.

Ashley Forster lives just down the street from the Halawis in a sky-blue house with white shutters. Since the arrest, she's passed the Halawi home on her bike every day after school and wondered why the paint on the front is peeling, why there's a gray and yellow stain on the second story that has never been washed off.

Before he was arrested, Mr. Halawi was always in the garage working on some machine. That was before Ashley's father told her to stop riding her bike by the Halawi house, when Ashley felt brave enough to stop and talk to Mr. Halawi once or twice.

"What are you building?" Ashley asked Mr. Halawi one day.

He turned to her, sweat beading up on his brown forehead. "Rebuilding an engine," he said.

But it didn't look like an engine to Ashley, and it made a scary noise when it backfired, like a bomb.

Ashley went home that day and told her father what she'd seen. "Does the engine in our car look like that, Dad?" she asked. "I've never seen one." But her father asked her what she thought it was, and Ashley told him it sounded like a bomb. So Mr. Forster started watching out the windows when the Halawis came and went, trying to see what Mr. Halawi was building in his garage.

One day, Mr. Forster didn't like the way Mr. Halawi glanced around him for coming cars, the way he looked jittery from lack of sleep, so Mr. Forster called a hotline to report suspicious activity.

A week after the call, Ashley rode her bike by the Halawi home again.

"Mr. Halawi," she asked, "What are you building an engine for?"

Mr. Halawi looked around, but the street was empty. "It's for Samira," he said. "Do you know her?"

Ashley laughed, screwing up her face. "She's in my class," she said, "but what does she need an engine for?"

Mr. Halawi smiled and pushed black hair out of his eyes. "A car," he said. "I'm rebuilding the engine so I can repair this car." He tossed his head back into the shadows of the garage. "I'm going to give her a car for her sixteenth birthday. But—" and he glanced at the road again—"it's a surprise. Don't tell her."

Ashley's eyes went wide. "A car?" she shuffled her feet, looking deeper into the garage as though other secrets were hidden inside. Before she turned away, she asked, "What color?"

"Red," Mr. Halawi said. "I'll paint it red. It's her favorite color." He turned back to the machine on the block, flitting around it like a hummingbird. "I'd better get back to work," he said, "before she gets home."

Officer Tom Carson was assigned to the case two hours after Mr. Forster's call. He'd been called back from a routine patrol, but he was late. He'd taken the patrol car to the hospital again. It was a quiet town, he'd reasoned. One or two missed traffic tickets wouldn't do anyone any harm.

Debriefing was quick and simple: suspected terrorist. 589 Tumbler Creek Street. They'd been getting more and more of these calls lately, but none ever amounted to much. Each arrest caused a minor neighborhood ruckus—then the case was quickly dismissed.

Tom was told to gather more evidence, talk to the neighbors. He was told to err on the side of caution. He was told to protect his country.

On his way to Tumbler Creek, Tom's son's face kept bubbling up in his mind. At the hospital, his son had been red, swollen, his head wide as a balloon. The doctors had put a shunt in three days ago, but the swelling wasn't coming down. His son still wasn't talking, and now his skull was red and soft and hairless.

Hydrocephaly, the doctor had called it. He'd told Tom it meant water in the skull. He'd told him it could be fatal.

Why not just call it what it is? Tom had wondered while he'd gripped his wife's fingers in his. The long medical name gave him no comfort.

Tom parked his patrol car on the curb and approached the Forsters' house. The Halawi home was dark and quiet, the curtains drawn.

When Tom knocked, a blonde woman in black leggings and a mustard tunic opened the door with a toddler in her arms.

"Afternoon, Ma'am," Tom said. He showed her his badge. "Is Mr. Forster home?"

"Oh no," she said. The child sucked on his mother's hair, peeking at Tom through eyes puffy with old tears. "He's at work until six."

"Would you mind if I came in and asked you a few questions?"

Mrs. Forster made Tom a cup of coffee and offered him crumb cake, which he refused. She told him Mr. Halawi had been friendly until three months ago.

"He's always hanging around in the garage," she said. "Never talks to anyone. Just comes down to work on some big piece of equipment, fiddling with his tools in the garage. Never goes out to run errands or go to work anymore. My husband is nervous. We used to let our daughter ride her bike by their house—but no more. Who knows what he might be working on?"

When they were finished, Mrs. Forster showed Tom to the door with her son in her arms. The child broke into a smile as Tom reached for the knob.

Mrs. Forster laughed. "I think he likes you," she said.

Tom followed the child's gaze. "I think he likes my patrol car," he said.

"Oh, sure," Mrs. Forster said. The toddler pulled at her blouse, setting a chubby hand on her collarbone. "He loves playing with toy cars. We give him fire trucks, police cars, all kinds of things. He's a real fanatic."

"Maybe he'll be a cop when he grows up," Tom said. He felt unusually happy, buoyed by something in the child's red face.

"Do you have any kids of your own, Officer?"

"One," Tom said. "Just one. A boy."

Crossing the lawn, something cracked in Tom's chest. He drove the patrol car around the block three times before he got on the highway. He parked the car beneath an overpass. Cars slowed as they passed him, glancing in their rearview mirrors to see if he would follow. He didn't issue any speeding tickets that afternoon. He pulled out his radar detector and set it in front of his face to hide his tears.

A week later, Tom arrested Mr. Nasir Halawi on suspicion of terrorist activities. A week after that, Samira Halawi's body arrived at the morgue, skull split, face red and swollen.

Water in the skull, Tom had thought then. *That's what killed her—the pain inside. Just like all of us.*

When her husband had been working a month on rebuilding the engine for Samira's birthday, Mrs. Leila Halawi had cornered him in the kitchen one morning after Samira had gone to school.

"Why don't you just let her use our car?" she'd asked. "How much longer will you be working on this thing, Nasir? Her birthday is next Thursday."

"I want her to have something special," he'd said. "Something of her own."

"But this is too much," Leila had said. "You've been down in that garage every day for a month. You have to rest. You have to get back on the job market. It's been three months since you were laid off."

"Some things are more important," Nasir had said. "Samira is one of them."

How differently things turned out, Leila thinks. She still can't understand the arrest, the trial, her husband's sudden departure—and then her daughter's.

Before Samira jumped from the overpass, Leila had struggled with the arrest herself. She'd wandered the house late at night in the week leading up to Samira's death, half sleepwalking, thinking her husband had gotten up to get a glass of water and forgotten to come back to bed. For a few moments every night, she'd expected to find him asleep on the couch with the television on.

On one of those nights, she'd stopped at the window. There was laughter outside, the thudding sound of something hitting the siding of the house. When she'd opened the kitchen window, a car had sped off.

Leila pinned her scarf over her hair and threw a shawl over her shoulders. She drifted down to the curb to survey the damage. There was a great patch of yellow and gray decorating the left side of the house, wet and shimmering under the moon.

"Mama?" Samira had followed her out into the driveway, shivering. "What is it?"

Leila shook her head. "I don't understand," she said.

"They egged our house," Samira said. "They egged us." But her voice was flat and quiet, and when she was done saying it she walked back into the house without a word.

Leila should have known then. She should have known something was wrong, if not that night, then when Samira came home from school with her head down, locking herself in her room. She should have known when Samira had started to chew her lips, her fingers, her pencils. She should have known the morning of Samira's birthday, when Samira refused to talk to her father when he called from prison. It was the last Thursday Leila would see her daughter alive.

"Come on, Mama," Samira had said from the bottom of the stairs, pretending she hadn't heard the phone. She was wearing her favorite red dress for her birthday, the one with the pleats and bows. "I'm late for homeroom."

That afternoon, on the way home from school, Samira threw herself from the overpass.

They held Nasir Halawi for two months, when he was acquitted on lack of evidence. No one could be sure how Samira's death had affected his trial, how it had turned suspicious hearts to pity.

Perhaps Mrs. LeBlanc got tired of finding black hairs jammed in the cracks in her windshield.

Perhaps Katerina Turner could no longer stand to say nothing.

Perhaps Ashley Forster was haunted by the chewed pencils Samira left in her desk.

Perhaps Samira's swollen face reminded Officer Carson too much of his son's.

The Friday after Samira's funeral, Leila sits in the garage with the doors open before she goes to prayer at the mosque, considering these things. She stares at the engine her husband never finished building.

The neighbors pass by. They stare. Leila doesn't look at them. She keeps her eyes on the engine, willing them to see her grief, daring them to accuse her, too.

The poem as a subway train

Nausheen Eusuf

does not sing. It does not delight or instruct.
It is not meant to be overheard. It shrills
along its subterranean channels, lurching
into the light of each temporary destination
and unsettling the rats along the tracks.

It is not sublime. There are no apparitions
like petals on a wet Parisian bough, only
the soot and filth of the city's bowels.
Strangers eye each other warily, yesterday's
papers litter the seats while plastic bottles roll
and beer cans rattle. And sometimes the lolling
of a head hanging from a strap—*did you—no—*

When it reaches the end of the line, it turns
right back, starts again, and keeps on going.

Contributors

Blaise Allen, PhD. She is a licensed clinical social worker, photojournalist, and Director of Community Outreach for the Palm Beach Poetry Festival. Her award winning poems have been widely published in literary anthologies and journals. Blaise bridges her passion of social welfare, imagery, and poetry, through community engagement in the arts: promoting voice, culture, and language arts education.

Kristy Athens is the author of *Get Your Pitchfork On!: The Real Dirt on Country Living* (Process Media, 2012). She has an MS in Food Systems and Society from Marylhurst University. Her nonfiction and short fiction have been published in a number of magazines, newspapers, and literary journals, and she has been a regular contributor to HandPicked Nation. Her text-infused, repurposed collage artwork is available at http://ithaka.etsy.com.

Morris Collins' first novel, *Horse Latitudes* (MP Publishing USA), was released in 2013 and will be reprinted in a second edition by Dzanc Books later this year. Other fiction and poetry has recently appeared in *Pleiades, Gulf Coast, The Chattahoochee Review, Michigan Quarterly Review*, and *Nimrod* among others. Morris lives in Boston and is a Visiting Assistant Professor of English at the College of the Holy Cross.

Asha Dore's work has recently appeared in *The Rumpus, Volume 1 Brooklyn, Hobart, LUMINA,* and elsewhere. Asha lives in Portland,

Oregon with her partner and three children where she is working on a book length critical lyric.

Nausheen Eusuf is a doctoral candidate in English at Boston University. She holds an MA from the Writing Seminars at Johns Hopkins, and her poetry has appeared in *Rattle, Southwest Review, Spillway, Poetry East, World Literature Today*, and other journals. Her chapbook *What Remains* was published by Longleaf Press at Methodist University.

Alexis Fedorjaczenko holds an MFA in Poetry & Nonfiction and an MPH in Health Policy. She has been published in *Naugatuck River Review* and in *Sentence: a Journal of Prose Poetics;* and she has attended residencies at the Vermont Studio Center, Elsewhere Studios, and Prairie Center for the Arts. She is currently on a yearlong U.S. travel adventure. When not on the road, Alexis makes her home on the east coast. She can also be found at: www.alexisgf.com

Ruth Foley lives in Massachusetts, where she teaches English for Wheaton College. Her work appears in numerous web and print journals, including *Antiphon, The Bellingham Review, and Sou'wester*. She is the author of two chapbooks, *Dear Turquoise* (dancing girl press) and *Creature Feature* (ELJ Publications), and serves as Managing Editor for Cider Press Review.

M.K. Foster's poetry has appeared or is forthcoming in *Gulf Coast; The Account; Sixth Finch; The Adroit Journal; Nashville Review; H.O.W. Journal; The Southeast Review; B O D Y;* and elsewhere and has been recognized with the 2013 Gulf Coast Poetry Prize, an Academy of

American Poets Prize, and two 2015 Pushcart Prize nominations. She holds an MFA from the University of Maryland and presently pursues a PhD at the University of Alabama.

A 4-time nominee for the Pushcart Prize, **Jonathan Greenhause** was longlisted for last year's National Poetry Competition by The Poetry Society, was a finalist for the 2015 *Aesthetica* Creative Writing Award, and was highly commended for *Southword Journal*'s 2016 Gregory O'Donoghue Poetry Prize. His poems have recently appeared or are forthcoming in *FOLIO, Green Mountains Review, RHINO,* and *Stand*, among others. This is his 3rd time appearing in *Clackamas Literary Review.*

Luke B. Goebel is the Prose Editor of *Autre Magazine.* He is a fiction writer who hails from Portland, Oregon. His first novel: *Fourteen stories, None of Them Are Yours,* was released in September of 2014 by FC2 as the winner of the Ronald Sukenick Prize for Innovative Fiction. He has work published in/at: *Tin House, Electric Literature, The American Reader, Pank, The New York Tyrant,* and elsewhere.

Meredith Hamilton lives and works in the Washington, DC, area but claims Durango, Colorado, as home. Her poetry has previously appeared in *Poet Lore.*

Toni Hanner's books are *The Ravelling Braid* (Tebot Bach, 2012), *Gertrude* (Traprock Books, 2012), and *The Book of Orange Dave* (chandeliergalaxy, 2015). Her poems may also be found in *Crab Creek Review, Southern Humanities Review,* and many other discerning publications.

Maya Hickman is a poet living in the Northwest. She finds inspiration in work with which she uses her hands, like making bread, and cooking. She believes in poetry and friendship.

Alex Andrew Hughes lives and works in Los Angeles. He splits his time, depending on his mood and the weather, between his training in clinical psychology, his research in existential crises, and his fiction, poetry, and sketching. Sometimes, however, he does absolutely nothing, and he enjoys that time the most. His poetry has appeared or is forthcoming in *Thin Air, Chiron Review*, and *Firewords Quarterly*.

Jamie Iredell is the author of four books, the most recent of which is *Last Mass*, a lyric essay about Catholicism, popular culture, and bears.

Michael Johnson is from Bella Coola, British Columbia. His poetry and essays have appeared in *The Southern Review, The Fiddlehead, Weber, Shenandoah*, and *The Malahat Review*, among others, and been selected for the Best American and Best Canadian poetry anthologies. His first collection *How to Be Eaten by a Lion* is forthcoming from Nightwood Editions. He works at a vineyard in Okanagan Falls.

J.M. Jones is a writer and editor from Philadelphia whose fiction and nonfiction have appeared recently or are forthcoming in *The Southeast Review, Barrelhouse, Phoebe*, and *The Normal School*. For more, please visit jasonmjones.net.

Cindy King's publications include work in *Callaloo, North American Review, American Literary Review, jubilat, Ruminate, Cortland Review, River Styx, Cimarron, Black Warrior, Barrow Street, The Pinch* and elsewhere. Her poetry can also be found online at weekendamerica. publicradio.org, rhinopoetry.org, and at the *Nashville Review*'s website. In 2014, she was awarded a Tennessee Williams Scholarship to attend the Sewanee Writers' Workshop. She has also received the Agha Shahid Ali Scholarship in Poetry from the Fine Arts Work Center in Provincetown. She currently lives in Lancaster, where she teaches at the University of North Texas at Dallas as an Assistant Professor of English.

Jen Knox's story collection, *After the Gazebo* (Rain Mountain Press), was nominated for the 2015 Pen/Faulkner Award. Some of her recent stories can be found in *The Adirondack Review, Crannóg Magazine, Gargoyle Magazine, Istanbul Review, PANK, Per Contra, Room Magazine,* and *The Saturday Evening Post.* Find Knox at: http://www.jenknox.com

Donald Levering's latest book, *Coltrane's God,* was published by Red Mountain Press in 2015. His previous book, *The Water Leveling with Us,* placed 2nd in the 2015 National Federation of Press Women Creative Verse Book Competition. Levering won the 2014 Literal Latté Award and was 1st Runner-Up for the Mark Fischer Prize in 2015. He lives in Santa Fe, New Mexico.

Jacob Lindberg lives in Minneapolis, MN. He works at the University of Minnesota-Twin Cities, and is completing his Masters of Fine Arts in Creative Writing at Hamline University in St. Paul, MN. He often reflects on and writes about his hometown Superior, WI, Lake Superior, and the people in this area. He sees flecks of God in the gut-wrenching, weeping, and oily things.

Jennifer Zeynab Maccani is a Syrian-American writer living in the greater Hershey, Pennsylvania area. Her short stories have recently appeared or are forthcoming in *Gulf Stream Literary Magazine, The Normal School, Mizna, Sukoon,* and elsewhere. She won an Honorable Mention Award in the Maine Review's 2015 Short Fiction Contest. She is currently at work on a novel and a collection of short stories.

Margaret Malone is the author of the story collection *People Like You,* selected as one of the best books of 2015 by *The Oregonian,* Powell's, The Quivering Pen, and the *Portland Mercury.* Her stories and essays can be found in *The Missouri Review, Oregon Humanities, Swink, Propeller Quarterly,* and elsewhere. She lives with her husband and two children in Portland, Oregon, where she is a co-host of the artist and literary gathering SHARE.

Todd McKie is an artist and writer whose stories have appeared in *PANK, Chicago Literati, Story Magazine Online, McSweeney's Internet Tendency,* and elsewhere. Todd lives in Boston.

Mary Miller is the author of two books: *Big World,* a story collection, and *The Last Days of California,* a novel. A forthcoming collection of stories, *Always Happy Hour,* will be published in 2017 by Liveright/Norton.

Stacey Allen Mills grew up with a pet rooster named Doughnut, finds sanctuary among the forests of the Pacific Northwest, and contemplates our journey across the plane of existence we all call life. His work often deals with themes of loss, loneliness, gender identity, and family violence. His art blurs the lines between nonfiction and fiction, between prose and poetry. Stacey is a degree candidate for an MFA in Creative Writing from Oregon State University—Cascades, and holds a Bachelor of Arts in English Literature and Writing from Marylhurst University.

Sonnet Mondal is the founder and editor in chief of *The Enchanting Verses Literary Review*. He has authored eight books of poetry and has performed on invitation at the Struga Poetry Evenings, Macedonia in 2014, Uskudar International Poetry Festival, Istanbul in 2015, and International Poetry Festival of Granada in 2016. He has been one of the featured writers at the International Writing Program at The University of Iowa and was featured as one of the Famous Five of Bengali Youths in *India Today* magazine in 2010. In March 2015, The CultureTrip website, London listed him among the Top Five Literary Entrepreneurs of Indian English Poetry. His works have appeared in the *Sheepshead Review, the McNeese Review, Two Thirds North, Penguin Review, Burning Word literary Journal, Oracle Fine Arts Review, Common Ground Review, The Adroit Journal, and Connotation Press* among others.

Jed Myers lives in Seattle. His poetry collections include *Watching the Perseids* (Sacramento Poetry Center Book Award) and the chapbook *The Nameless* (Finishing Line Press). His work has received Southern Indiana Review's Editors' Award, the Literal Latte Poetry Award, and Blue Lyra Review's Longish Poem Award. His poems have appeared in *Prairie Schooner, Nimrod, Crab Orchard Review, Harpur Palate, Crab Creek Review, The Briar Cliff Review, Atlanta Review, Quiddity,* and elsewhere.

Robert Nazarene founded MARGIE / The American Journal of Poetry and IntuiT House Poetry Series, where he received a publishers' National Book Critics Circle award in poetry (2006). His first volume of poems is *CHURCH* (2006). A new collection, *Bird In The Street,* is new in 2016. His poems have Appeared in *AGNI, Callaloo, The Iowa Review, The Journal of the American Medical Association, Ploughshares, Plume, Salmagundi, STAND (UK),* and elsewhere. He was educated at The McDonough School of Business at Georgetown University.

Randolph Parker makes his living as a marketing and advertising writer in Memphis. His work has appeared in *The Southern Poetry Anthology* (Texas Review Press, 2013), *Tidal Basin Review, Grey Sparrow, Barely South, Avatar Review,* and other publications.

Ricardo Pau-Llosa's seventh book of poems, *Man* (2014), is from Carnegie Mellon U Press as were his previous four titles. He is also an art critic and curator.

Paulann Petersen, Oregon Poet Laureate Emerita, has six full-length books of poetry, most recently *Understory,* from Lost Horse Press in 2013. Her poems have appeared in many journals and anthologies, including *Poetry, The New Republic, Prairie Schooner, Willow Springs, Calyx,* and the *Internet's Poetry Daily.* She was a Stegner Fellow at Stanford University, and the recipient of the 2006 Holbrook Award from Oregon Literary Arts. In 2013 she received Willamette Writers' Distinguished Northwest Writer Award.

Having retired to write poetry in Naples, Florida, Dr. **Oliver Rice** has won the Theodore Roethke Prize and twice been nominated for a Pushcart Prize. His poems have appeared widely in literary journals and anthologies in the United States, as well as in Canada, England, Austria, Turkey, and India.

Matthew Robinson's words have appeared at *Word Riot, Nailed Magazine, O-Dark-Thirty,* and elsewhere; and in the short story anthology *The Night, and the Rain, and the River* published by Forest Avenue press. He received his MFA in creative writing from Portland State University and lives and writes in Portland, Oregon.

Ruben Rodriguez writes, paints, and wastes his time at the foot of the San Bernardino Mountains. He is the fiction editor of *The Great American Lit Mag* and author of the chapbook *We Do What We Want* (Orange Monkey Publishing, 2015). His poems have been deemed fit for consumption by the likes of *Driftwood Press, Hawai'i Review, Oxford Magazine, Welter, 94 Creations, Perceptions,* and others. You can find him at www.rubenstuff.com.

Frank Rossini grew up in New York City & moved to Eugene, Oregon, in 1972. A graduate of the MFA program in Creative Writing at the University of Oregon, he taught for forty-three years. He has published poems in various journals including *The Seattle Review, Windfall, Raven Chronicles,* and *Mas Tequila Review.* His book of poems, *midnight the blues,* was published by sight|for|sight books in 2013.

Mike Salisbury's fiction has appeared in *Avery Anthology, Black Warrior Review,* and *Crab Orchard Review,* among others. Mike is a recent graduate of the MFA program at Pacific University. He lives with his wife and daughter along Michigan's West Coast.

Cameron Schott is from Sarasota, Florida and has been writing for most of his life. He is a sophomore at Palm Beach Atlantic University, where he is pursuing a Bachelor of Arts in communication with a minor in creative writing.

Adam Tavel won the Permafrost Book Prize for Plash & Levitation (University of Alaska Press, 2015). He is also the author of *The Fawn Abyss* (Salmon Poetry, 2016). His recent poems appear, or will soon appear, in *Southwest Review, Beloit Poetry Journal, The Gettysburg Review, The Emerson Review, Sycamore Review, Spoon River Poetry Review,* and *Tar River Poetry,* among others. He is a professor of English at Wor-Wic Community College and the reviews editor for *Plume.* You can find him at http://adamtavel. com.

Ed Taylor is the author of the novel *Theo,* the poetry collection *Idiogest,* and the poetry chapbook *The Rubaiyat of Hazmat.* His work has most recently appeared in *New World Writing* and *Southern Poetry Review* and is forthcoming in *St Petersburg Review, The Literary Review,* and *Gargoyle.*

Katie Todd is an artist, mother, healer, and co-founder of Galactivations.com, an online global boutique of energetic and astrological insight. She creates space, possibility, and magic from her home base in Portland, Oregon. You can find her online at KatieToddArt.com.

James Valvis has placed poems or stories in *Arts & Letters, Barrow Street, Clackamas Literary Review, Ploughshares, River Styx, The Sun,* and many others. His poetry was featured in *Verse Daily.* His fiction was chosen for Sundress Best of the Net. A former US Army soldier, he lives near Seattle.

Dennis Vanvick is a retired, self-employed technical consultant. He winters among the eight million inhabitants of Bogota, Colombia, and summers amongst the flora and fauna of northwest Wisconsin. Many of his short stories and essays have appeared in print journals and on the web. He can be reached at vanvikd@hotmail.com.

Dov Weinman has previously published poetry in the *Whitefish Review* and *Poetica Magazine* and recently finished an MS in environmental studies at the University of Montana. He currently lives in the Philippines as a Coastal Resource Management Peace Corps Volunteer.

John Sibley Williams is the editor of two Northwest poetry anthologies and the author of nine collections, including *Controlled Hallucinations* (2013) and *Disinheritance* (forthcoming 2016). A five-time Pushcart nominee and winner of the American Literary Review Poetry Contest and Vallum Award for Poetry, John serves as editor of *The Inflectionist Review* and works as a literary agent. Previous publishing credits include: *The Midwest Quarterly, december, Third Coast, Baltimore Review, Nimrod International Journal, Hotel Amerika, Rio Grande Review, Inkwell, Cider Press Review, Bryant Literary Review, RHINO,* and various anthologies. He lives in Milwaukie, Oregon.

Joan Wilking's fiction has appeared in *The Atlantic, The Barcelona Review, Other Voices, The Pacifica Review, Ascent, New World Writing, Hobart, Night Train, Punchnels* and many other publications online and in print. Her creative nonfiction and essays have appeared in *Brevity, New World Writing,* and *The Manifest Station.* Her short story, "Deer Season," was a prize-winning finalist for the The *Chicago Tribune*'s 2010 Nelson Algren Award. Her story, "Clutter," published in the *Elm Leaves Journal,* received a special mention in the 2016 Pushcart Prize Anthology.

Andrea Wyatt is the author of three poetry collections. Her work has appeared or is forthcoming in *Copperfield Review, Gargoyle,* and *Gravel.* Wyatt's poem *Sunday Morning Gingerbread* was nominated for a 2015 Pushcart. She works for the National Park Service in Washington, DC, and is associate editor of poetry journal *By&By.*

A.R. Zarif is originally from Chicago and is an undergraduate at New York University. His work has appeared in *Hartskill Review, London Journal of Fiction,* and *Bear Review.*

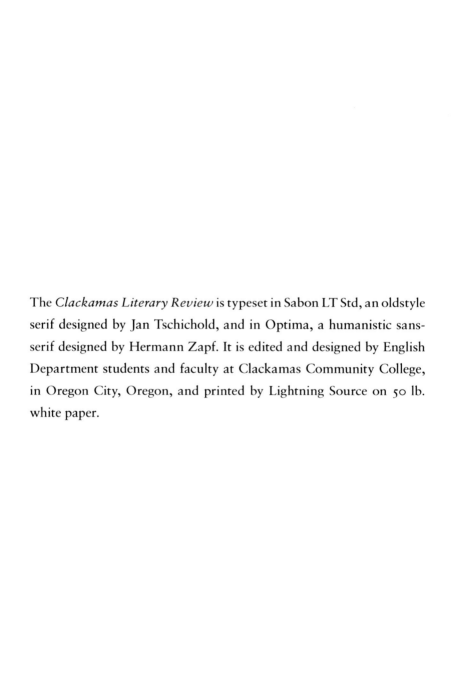

The *Clackamas Literary Review* is typeset in Sabon LT Std, an oldstyle serif designed by Jan Tschichold, and in Optima, a humanistic sans-serif designed by Hermann Zapf. It is edited and designed by English Department students and faculty at Clackamas Community College, in Oregon City, Oregon, and printed by Lightning Source on 50 lb. white paper.

Visit

CLACKAMAS LITERARY REVIEW

clackamasliteraryreview.org
clackamasliteraryreview.submittable.com
facebook.com/clackamasliteraryreview

Contact
clr@clackamas.edu

CLACKAMAS LITERARY REVIEW

the finest writing for the best readers

Clackamas Literary Review has been committed to publishing quality writing from around the world since 1997. Use the form below or visit us on Submittable to receive the latest and forthcoming issues.

Clackamas Literary Review

	1 year	$10
_____	2 years	$18
	3 years	$26

Name _____

Address _____

City / State / Zip _____

Email _____

Send this form and check or money order to:

Clackamas Literary Review
English Department
Clackamas Community College
19600 Molalla Avenue
Oregon City, Oregon 97045

CPSIA information can be obtained
at www.ICGtesting.com
Printed in the USA
FSOW02n0418250316
18413FS

9 780979 688287